'Richard Cornish is a respected food writer with impressive research skills as well as an appreciative palate. In deciding to forgo meat (and fish and poultry) for one year he also decided to investigate the realities of all types of farming today, as well as to highlight how to have a great food life as a non-meat eater. He has written a fascinating and discursive investigation into flavour, skill, traditional knowledge, the importance of *"terroir"*, and confronts the reader with the true cost of quality. His enthusiasm for the produce from his own garden or that from the gardens of other enthusiasts is inspiring and infectious and he convincingly makes the case that we would all be healthier if we ate more plant foods and that if we do decide to eat meat, we should choose it carefully.'

Stephanie Alexander

MY YEAR without MEAT

RICHARD CORNISH

MELBOURNE
UNIVERSITY
PRESS

This book is dedicated to the farmers who grow our food,
without whom we would starve to death.

MELBOURNE UNIVERSITY PRESS
An imprint of Melbourne University Publishing Limited
11–15 Argyle Place South, Carlton, Victoria 3053, Australia
mup-info@unimelb.edu.au
www.mup.com.au

First published 2016
Text © Richard Cornish, 2016
Design and typography © Melbourne University Publishing Limited, 2016

Text design and typesetting by Megan Ellis
Cover design by Philip Campbell Design
Printed in Australia by McPherson's Printing Group

National Library of Australia Cataloguing-in-Publication entry

Cornish, Richard, 1967—author.

My year without meat/Richard Cornish.

9780522864113 (paperback)
9780522864120 (ebook)

Vegetarianism—Health aspects.
Vegetarian cooking.
Food industry and trade—Moral and ethical aspects.

613.262

Contents

1

The Roadside Revelation for Mr Meat

I knew I had a problem with meat when I found myself eating a roast shoulder of lamb on the bonnet of my HiLux ute on a lonely country road.

I was returning home after staying with an old friend on a farm perched on the side of an extinct volcano. I was finishing writing a book at the time, and in return for the use of a small shed with a view over several valleys and a mountain range beyond, I cooked the evening meals. It was midwinter and as usual the meals were anchored around the central dish of meat. A solar system of lesser vegetable dishes and condiments orbiting a massive fat star of animal protein at its core. Chook stuffed with bacon. Corned beef. Sausages. And then an entire forequarter of lamb that had been slow roasting on a bed of garden rosemary and garlic grown in the deep red volcanic earth. The forequarter, complete with shank, had been butchered in a rudimentary manner; from the shoulder continued a long but truncated neck. It was to be dinner that night but a call from home to help with a daughter with the flu had me stuffing my clothes into my bag and reference books back into boxes. I jumped into the ute.

'I can't eat all this,' said my friend, carrying the baking tray of hot lamb fresh from the oven, mitts protecting her hands from the heat. 'Take this back to feed the missus and the girls,' she said. Laying an old copy of *The Weekly Times* down to protect the seat, she then placed the hot lamb, wrapped like a chrysalis in cling film, and slid the seatbelt over it as a little humorous visual coda to my visit. 'I have had enough meat this week,' she added, before patting the roof of the ute to send us both on our way. My lamb and me.

The crushed red-rock road gave way to blacktop bitumen, a thin line of black weaving between giant white gums. Sheep grazed in the paddocks on the other side of the roadway tree line, their hot breath forming pillows of white steam in the last light of the dying winter sun. The forest gave way to open country, grim, stony and cold. My meaty travelling companion sat silent but still hot next to me. Rivulets of condensed moisture ran down the inside of the plastic. The warm aroma of browned meat had escaped through gaps in the wrapping and filled the cabin. It had been some time since lunch, and home in the city was hours away. With the nail on my index finger I pierced the plastic and together with my thumb pincered off a strip of crisp dark-brown meat from along the neck. It was salty, crunchy with intensely concentrated flavour. The first strip was soon followed by another. The bands of muscle below these, although sweeter and moister, hadn't been as denatured by heat and had more resilience. The deeper I delved the more the lamb muscles became stronger than those in my hands. Unable to gain greater purchase with my left hand alone I pulled over, one wheel on the gravel, the other on the brown grass. What happened next might offend faint-hearted readers.

The crown of the road had been made quite steep to drain away water in this flat plateau, so the ute was tilting to one side, making it quite difficult and uncomfortable to reach across to tear away another piece of meat. I unbuckled both my seatbelt and the lamb's and took the still-warm roasting tray, placing it on the bonnet of the HiLux. I tore away the plastic and sunk two fingers into the shoulderblade to make a void. Spreading my fingers apart I created an opening. From this I could pull a tranche of muscles from the shoulderblade. Hardworking muscles that lifted the sheep's head up and down during its life: they were long and coarse, sweet and carrying the lanolic aroma of a merino crossbreed. Further down the leg, the deep-bronze meaty chunks from the lower leg were well done, the muscle fibres collapsing without resistance, the protein in the tendon cooked away to an unctuous jelly. The layer of fat towards the flank was crisp, brown and salty. From down the road the sound of a diesel engine rapidly changing down gears broke the stuporous bonnet-top gorging. I looked up to see a high-school bus carefully crawling past my stopped ute, the fresh-faced students looking on passively at what I can only imagine was a truly disturbing sight: a large middle-aged man standing by the side of the road gnawing on the still-articulated shoulder of a sheep. The bus edged away. I looked down. I had eaten most of the exterior muscles on the lamb. There were brown, sticky, caramelised cooking juices around my mouth and some of the once-liquid fat now congealed on the bull bar. The red tail-lights of the bus danced in the distance as the homeward-bound bus bounced on the poorly maintained road. The red dots dipped and rose one more time before they disappeared around a bend. The cold wind set the fat and meat juices on the skin solid. It was then that I realised I had a real issue with meat and it needed further investigation.

A few days later, Jane Willson, then editor of *Epicure*, the weekly food, wine and dining lift-out of Fairfax Media's *The Age*, called. I was a regular contributor. We talked about a story on the global rise of the profile of vegetables. I was the section's unofficial 'meat editor', so dubbed by the previous editor, Veronica Ridge, as she was a lifelong vegetarian and depended on me for meat matters. I had form in this area. I had written an article on rare-breed lamb for the now-defunct *Divine Food and Wine* magazine. It involved lining up carcasses of a dozen rare sheep breeds and tasting five cuts from each animal. In the end we all consumed around 3 kilograms of lamb. At *Epicure* we also established the annual Christmas-ham-tasting story to find the best ham in the nation. The same was instituted for the best chickens and other meats. If there was a meat story I was your man.

The vegetable story was prompted by a confluence of changes in cooking worldwide. Continuing blows in Europe from the global financial crisis (GFC) were reshaping the way diners were eating and what they were willing to pay for a meal. Chefs needed to drop prices but where would the cuts be made? Staff? Electricity? The expensive and ongoing laundry costs to keep white linen on tables? The canny chefs of Europe were turning to their traditional cultures and taking humble vegetable-based peasant dishes and polishing them up with an urbane flourish, putting small amounts of exquisite mushrooms and hand-podded baby beans on designer plates and lapping them with a sauce created by reducing the stock made with a single ham bone. It wasn't vegetarian but neither was it meat. Two great Australian chefs, Annie Smithers and Matt Wilkinson, had just produced books that were basically paeans to growing and cooking vegetables. Hugh Fearnley-Whittingstall, the double-barrel named, fop-haired food hippy of *River Cottage* TV and book fame, had undergone an onscreen road to Damascus transformation that was to set the zeitgeist. He had famously cut his hair and eschewed meat in favour of meals made entirely from his own homegrown vegetables.

There was a lot of chatter on social media and from the far-left animal protection groups about giving up meat altogether, or just once a week. This followed Paul McCartney's online video where he performs *Meat free Monday/It's a fun day/And it's happening all around the world.* The song is deliberately lamentable, with McCartney addressing the camera: 'You can do better than that! Send your songs to Meat Free Monday'. I don't sing.

Jane and I worked and reworked the concept of a cover story on the rise of vegetables. Plant Matters. Plant Kingdom Rules. Looking Up to Vegetables. No matter how we worked the words for the cover, the story didn't seem to be strong enough. Then we considered an exercise in immersion journalism, where the writer enters the world of the topic and becomes the eyes, ears and other sensory organs of the reader, and reports back what they experience. I had previously imposed a similar experiment on my family for the sake of a story on a trend starting in the San Francisco Bay Area called The 100-Mile Diet. For several weeks we were only allowed to eat food that had been grown within 160 kilometres of our suburban home. It was fascinating for me. Less so for the kids. I found a beekeeper several blocks away, and a traditional fishing family who caught fish in the bay using a technique that had been around since biblical times. They sold their fish from their humble home that over the years had become surrounded by gleaming steel and concrete bayside apartments.

Here we were again. 'Mr Meat,' said Jane. 'Can you give up flesh for a few weeks?'

'That's like a smoker going without a ciggie for a few days,' I replied. 'Not desirable but very easy to achieve. Let's make it a month.' It was a deal. I would not eat meat for a month and would explore the world from a vegetarian's perspective.

'Good,' said Jane. 'I need copy in five weeks' time.'

AN EXAMINATION OF A LIFE IN MEAT

The train trip home seemed unusually long. I was running over the logistics. Ostensibly it was easy. Just don't eat meat. Meat, poultry and fish. They were the ground rules. I double-checked the dictionary apps on my iPhone to make sure I could still have a cafe latte, omelette and washed rind cheese. 'A vegetarian is a person who mainly eats food from plants. They also eat some foods from animals such as cheese and eggs but never flesh. This includes sea creatures.' I hadn't signed up to be a vegan—'a person who only eats food produced by plants and not by or from animals or insects'. Which includes honey from bees.

Going through my diary, however, revealed that my little story experiment had a few snags. Literally. In a few weeks I was due to host an international $400-a-ticket outdoor BBQ festival with some of the hottest chefs in the world appearing as guests. Shortly after that I had also committed to judge a sausage competition at a country show. This was no ordinary show. This was the Red Hill Show—the country show I had grown up with in the green rolling hills of the Mornington Peninsula, south of Melbourne. It was the biggest event on my childhood calendar, even bigger than Christmas. The show was already being advertised and my appearance had made the local newspapers. Of this my mother was amazingly proud. Although she had previously brushed aside my hubristic announcement that a cookbook I had co-written had made *The New York Times* Best Cookbook of the Year list, she was openly boasting about my involvement with the local sausage competition. My older brother, a country bloke with dust-dry wit, nailed it when he said, 'Mother's friends read the local newspaper. They don't read *The New York Times*.'

So there lay the conundrum at the very heart of this experiment. Was I becoming a vegetarian or simply playing the part of one? Was it more like an agent going deep undercover, spending a month as an avatar, living in a skin constructed and not grown? I had to respect the readers, colleagues and people who already followed meat-free diets but I also had commitments I had to keep.

I decided on some rules and boundaries for my experiment and the story. I was a meat eater who had given up meat to see what it was like. And like a Catholic during the Renaissance I could buy indulgences where absolutely necessary for professional considerations. As for the sausage judging? I would simply not swallow. The train drew to a stop. It was almost empty. The few remaining passengers got off and sunken-eyed, grey-skinned youths swarmed through the doors. I had missed my stop, this was Frankston. The end of the line.

THE FLESH COLLECTOR

Back home the freezer was an icy library of meat. Stacked on end, side by side were carefully labelled, vacuumed-packed pieces of meat from different cows, pigs, sheep, birds, fish and wild animals. My love of great meat was evangelistic. The meat that I knew and loved came from rare-breed, grass-fed, pampered and loved animals. Meat that could be marbled like the best Carrara from animals raised with husbandry that would make the hospitality at the Park Hyatt look like a backpackers.

Travelling the countryside with a fiberglass cool box in the back of the ute, I bought and collected the best meat I could lay my hands on. This was a habit I had picked up as soon as I got my licence. Armed with a 35-millimetre camera I was given for my eighteenth birthday, I travelled to the country at weekends, taking photographs of old buildings and the people I met. I would buy honey, a sweet souvenir of the bush in which the bees foraged. I would buy meat from different butchers who had access to different herds of beef and flocks of lambs. With them I could compare and contrast the flavour. It was an edible education.

I shared these benchmarks with friends and respected chefs, showing them how good meat could taste, passing on the details of the farmers and butchers. The quality of great meat doesn't survive in a freezer for longer than two months and the amount of meat I had collected way surpassed my ability to consume it once my month without meat had finished. With a heavy heart I handed over my icy meat collection to friends and colleagues. To my mate with whom I co-owned a sausage mincer I gave a shoulder of lamb from a Shropshire ewe that had grazed on native grass-seed heads. To my neighbour, a wine writer, I donated a pork belly from a Berkshire gilt that had grazed by the banks of the Murray and been fed on lupin seeds and avocados. To other friends and colleagues I bequeathed vacuum-packed wild quails, hand-caught tuna belly, and rump steak from a 6-year-old grass-fed steer.

The last steak in the collection was a well-marbled porterhouse. Grass fed and dry aged for thirty days this was to be my last meat supper for a month. Defrosted and grill ready, the steak let out a little bloody juice before it hit the hot steel. Seared, turned, rested and sliced, it was a truly magnificent piece of beef. It had been sliced from the carcass of a 3-year-old Belted Galloway, a lowland Scottish breed that has shaggy black coats with a great band of white hair strapped around their midriffs. Truly magnificent beasts. Mostly even tempered, the mothers become extremely protective of their calves and therefore are suited to range freely and widely and fatten on the hard country of the hills. They are perfectly capable of fending off a fox with one fell swoop of their thick, bony heads. I chewed the flesh, which was in no way tough but yielded to the tooth with the perfect amount of resistance. The fat had marbled beautifully and was not only making the meat moist but also offering a richness that only grass-fed beef fat gives, a clean finishing sensation on the palate. There was something in the aroma, a sweetness. The sweetness of fresh grass. The same smell you get when close to a cow. Cows have the same sweet smell of grass on their breath. The thought then struck me: somehow this cow had captured that ethereal quality and preserved it in its flesh.

I lit the charcoal grill outside. It's basically a steel box on legs. You put charcoal in it, light the charcoal, wait until the flames recede and then cook the meat over the dying embers. I am such a meat snob that I won't use firelighters, as they make the meat taste like a petrol station. To get the fire going I supercharge the flames with a stream of air by plugging the vacuum cleaner hose into the exhaust. I cooked the steak slowly, carefully creating cross-hatched sear lines on the steak by regularly turning the meat 90 degrees so no one side fires out. Cooked to medium rare I let the meat rest for 12 minutes, sliced it and served it to the family. I chewed it slowly, making the most of every movement of my jaw. The steak was juicy, sweet, with a clean tangy finish. I knew that steak was the last piece of meat I was going to eat for some time.

2

Who Let the Pigs In?

It was Christmas Eve about forty years ago and Mum and her best friend were plucking chickens. I was a kid, playing in the garden; the sweet smell of virgilia blossom hung in the warm summer air. Mum and Aunty Sue were perched on kitchen chairs in the shade of the trees. (I called her Aunty Sue although we were no relation, because that was a time when kids didn't call adults by their first names. It was less a compromise than a mark of respect and emotional closeness. I still call her Aunty Sue). The women were hunched over buckets of steaming hot water. Pulling small fistfuls of feathers away from the skin in the direction of the chickens' still intact heads without damaging the skin was a skill. The freshly killed chicken had a sweet smell intensified by the hot water and the steam coming off the skin.

We were farmers. We had a dairy; Aunty Sue and Uncle John had recently given up theirs to raise sheep. We all kept chickens for eggs. On special occasions we would kill a few. The ladies would watch their flock and look out for the one with the fullest breast, the widest gait and the fullest crop. They wanted a nice plump bird that was towards the top of the pecking order. A hen-pecked bird would be stressed and tough, and a tough bird wouldn't cut the mustard on the Christmas dinner table. A quick twist of the neck with a deft flick of the wrist and the bird's lights were out. The ladies didn't go in for the dramatic bloodletting of the hatchet and the cutting block. The killing was traumatic enough for these animal-loving ladies without adding blades and blood.

Roast chook was something special. Discussions were had as to the best way to cook them and phone calls were put in to mothers and fathers for advice. Back then chook for us was as commonplace as turkey or pheasant is for today's cook—a rarely attempted dish, saved for the most special of occasions.

Then came the change. We noticed the trucks first. Great feed trucks. Huge, shiny white trucks full of chicken feed that roared around our country roads. While the milk tankers, laden with tons of liquid, crawled at a snail's pace up the winding hills, this new breed of heavy movers travelled at speed on our roads, their drivers not afraid or not aware that they were crossing the white line. The term 'being taken out by a feed truck' entered the local lexicon. Our friends who had been dairy farmers sold their old herds and erected chicken sheds. These were long squat sheds fabricated from cement sheeting and, despite the green rolling hills and lush pastures on which they were built, were painted a nature-defiling shade of undercoat pink. They sprung up around the countryside in clusters. On a still summer's day the fetid funk of ammonia emanating from the sheds filled the once-sweet air. It was fun visiting a friend's chicken sheds when the newly hatched chicks were delivered, thousands at a time, corralled together for warmth by a low solid fence of cardboard. We picked them up by the armful, fluffy yellow cheeping balls. As the weeks went on and the birds lost their down and grew feathers they were no longer cute but ugly adolescents, standing on caked beds of rice husks, wet with their own faeces, fallen birds flattened and mummified in the corners. A heatwave could wipe out the population of an entire poorly ventilated shed. Then we were called in to help with the morbid task of throwing thousands of birds into a hastily dug pit. We quickly discovered that factory farming wasn't nice. It wasn't pretty. It was a stinking affair. However, we couldn't help but notice the farmers who got out of cows and sheep and into raising poultry for meat were the ones driving new cars.

Only a few years earlier, too early for me to remember, our family had got out of pig farming. We had been dairy farmers selling cream to the factory. The skim milk was mixed with grain and fed to the pigs. When we started selling whole milk we got rid of the pigs. Across the countryside little pig growers like us were closing down. Pigs were no longer being raised outdoors but in sheds just as the chickens were. A lyrical version of this exodus from 'outside in' is told in the lives of the Nehill brothers, who lived in the rolling hills at South Purrumbete near the Otway Ranges in Victoria's green south-west. Three bachelor brothers—Alex, Joe and Peter Nehill—were raising pigs throughout the first part of the twentieth century. They farmed with draught horses until 1978. They had a herd of dairy cows that they milked by hand, selling the cream—as we did—and feeding the skim milk to the pigs.

English Large Black pigs have black skin and hair that protects them from the sun, and their generous covering of fat keeps them warm in winter. The Nehill brothers' big old boar was called Paddy and he lived in a sty made of hand-hewn hardwood and half a corrugated-iron water tank. When he wasn't fathering piglets he spent his time lying in the shade of an old apple tree. But there was to be no future for Paddy and the Nehill Brothers. Pig sheds replaced green paddocks and lean, white pigs superseded the fat black ones. The brothers were already elderly when Paddy died in 2002. With Paddy gone it was the end of an era. He was one of the last pigs of his breed in the nation. To continue the pig farming business, Alex, the last surviving brother, would have to interbreed brother pigs with their sisters, and fathers with their daughters. Interbred animals don't have vigour and are prone to both congenital deformities and chronic illness. An old man himself, Alex chose to end 130 years of family pig farming and allow the last of his sows to live out their lives on the farm.

The way the Nehills farmed, in close contact with a small herd, allowed them to assess their animals' health, behaviour and readiness for slaughter. This deep cultural understanding of animal husbandry and commerciality was lost when the animals we eat moved en masse from the outdoors to indoors, from small herds and flocks to large-scale commercial enterprises. Our relationship with the animals we eat changed forever. At the same time it meant forcing animals to change the way they lived to provide us with meat. It also meant the way we consume meat changed significantly.

The big pink chicken sheds were always called chicken sheds. Never chook sheds. That diminutive and familiar word, chook, was left to the household egg flock. After they were built and the feed trucks came down our roads, Mum would buy frozen chickens in bags from the supermarket. She and Aunty Sue were glad they never had to pluck a chicken again. With the responsibility for taking an animal's life out of her hands, Mum was more willing and more able to cook chicken. If it was discounted at the supermarket we would be even more likely to see it on the table. From being the dense, flavoursome, almost dark meat with strong sweet poultry aromas we knew and ate a few times a year, chicken changed to being cheap, white and mealy, with bones you could bend with your bare hands. In what seemed the blink of an eye, chicken went from being a food reserved for the annual ritual feast of Christmas, to being a body shrink-wrapped in a bag with a big red sticker on it. Chicken went from something special to being on special. In Mum's lifetime, chicken consumption has increased tenfold, from under 5 kilograms per person per annum to close to 50 kilograms. In that same time, lamb and mutton consumption has decreased threefold to just over 10 kilograms per person a year. Chicken is cheap. Lamb is dear.

It wasn't until I decided to stop eating meat that I realised just how ubiquitous chicken, bacon, ham, preserved and fresh meat had become in the Australian diet and other Western nations. It forced me to confront how narrow meat-free food choices are for those living in the everyday world. We are drowning in a sea of animal products and it takes good navigation to chart a course for a healthy diet without them. It threw me the challenge of creating a new way of eating. It revealed that we live in a society almost devoid of animal compassion, and contempt for those who make the choice not to put meat into their mouths.

I knew this couldn't be a hunter-gatherer affair. I prefer not to use the term 'Paleo' as it has lost its meaning. (The modern diet would have been as familiar to our lithic forebears as Foxtel iQ or anything in the Innovations catalogue. In his book *Dark Emu*, Indigenous Australian author Bruce Pascoe points out that grinding tools were used to grind grain into meal 30 000 years before the Egyptians and that fermented bread was being made by inland tribes at the time of the first contact with Europeans.) I do not have time to kill my own prey. I am a freelance writer and therefore any spare moment not spent typing is spent looking after my family or drinking. Or both. I have killed animals in the past. I have wrung the necks of chickens and rabbits and killed other farm animals for food. That is something that was not going to be part of this journey.

I wanted to see what the changes were in raising animals for food from when I was a lad and to see if there were any morally and ethically acceptable farming practices for those who do eat meat. So much had changed in my life since roast chicken was something that was celebrated. That brought people together to watch as the oldest person in the family, often the grandfather, was called upon to carve. At Christmas this was left to my maternal grandfather. He would roll up his sleeves and do with the knife and carving fork what I thought were religious gestures over the bird. He was in fact, I was to learn later, doing a bit of air carving, rehearsing his moves without making a mark. Carving a chook wasn't commonplace. It was an annual event, so he had to take time to recall the muscle memory. When the chicken was served it would arrive at the table of seated diners and be presented like a special guest artist—with a flourish and an introduction. And at that point we would bow our heads and say grace. *For what we are about to receive/May the Lord make us truly thankful/Amen.*

And we were truly thankful.

3

Country Pasty Nazi

Working as a freelancer covering food trends takes me across the country. My first day as a newly minted meat-free food writer saw me on an assignment interviewing and photographing a farmer raising a rare breed of cattle. The interview was a little odd. I did the interview and took the photographs, but the conversation around the way those amazing white cattle with black noses would taste on the BBQ fell flat. The grower was more interested in the aesthetics of his animals on his bijou property than the way they would taste. Even though they had contacted the paper, promoting their cattle as an old English beef breed, the owners seemed more interested in the way they would photograph.

As I headed out to the location that day for my appointment with the farmer, I reached the main street of a small central Victorian town just as I was starting to think about lunch. The smell of baking pastry wafting from the bakery made me hit the brakes. It was a stock-standard, old-fashioned country bakery. The walls and high ceiling of the old goldfields building had once been painted an inoffensive shade of cream that had darkened to gold over the years with the heat from the ovens.

A fluorescent tube on the roof cast cold green light at the back of the bakery. A lone, pasty-faced baker watched me with obvious impatience as I scanned the chalkboard menu for choices. The baker had seen too many early starts, not enough sun and, going by the slight tremor in his hands, the interior of too many depressing country pubs. There were steak pies; steak and bacon pies; steak and kidney pies; steak, bacon and cheese pies; chicken pies; curried chicken pies; chicken and bacon pies; and, thankfully, a vegetarian pie.

'Excuse me,' I said. 'What's in the vegetarian pie?'

'Cauliflower and broccoli in cheese sauce,' answered the baker.

'I'll have one of those, please,' I answered.

'Don't make them anymore,' he said. 'Not very popular.'

'Oh,' I replied. 'What do you have for vegetarians?'

'Pasties,' was the answer.

I bought one, with a sachet of sauce, and sat on a bench in the small park opposite the shop. I pulled out the pasty from the white paper bag. It was a traditional Cornish pasty with thick short pastry and a seam running down the centre on top. I waited a while, to let it cool down a little, squirted sauce parallel to the seam and took a bite. The reason why it looked so much like a traditional Cornish pasty was because it was a traditional Cornish pasty, made with swede, potato and beef. Beef! Gristly beef. Beef with great chunks of ground tendon. I was indignant. Not about the meat but that I had, perhaps, been lied to. I spat the mouthful of pastry, root vegetables and meat onto the ground, attracting a small flock of pushy pigeons. With them squawking over their gristly meal I returned to the baker, assuming there had been an error.

The baker was reading the paper and looked up, impatient. I asked him if there had been a mistake. Perhaps he had meant to give me a vegetarian pasty instead of one with meat in it.

'Well, it's got mostly vegetables in it,' came the reply. It wasn't just ignorant or rude. It was contemptuous. I looked him in the eye then looked up to the menu board for other meat-free lunch options. The sandwiches were all premade, wrapped tightly in cling film, the filling between the slices of white bread identified by an alphabetic code written in blue permanent marker. HCT—ham, cheese and tomato. CAM—chicken, avocado and mayonnaise. Every sandwich and pie was made with meat. The egg filling in the egg and lettuce sandwiches was made with egg, lettuce, mayo and bacon. Even the bread rolls had bacon on them. This place was a temple to flesh. I asked for a bread and butter roll. The baker wouldn't cut and butter it for me as all the sandwiches were premade in the morning and the 'girl' had already gone home for the day.

I sat in the park with a dry bread roll in a brown paper bag, surrounded by a few expectant pigeons.

Timing is everything. It was only later that I realised I may have put myself in a difficult position. I had agreed with Jane Willson that I was no longer eating meat. In doing so, I had overlooked the fact that I had also agreed to take on a role as part of the Melbourne Food and Wine Festival, which involved three weeks of celebrations around the city. The main event was to be a day-long BBQ masterclass, with famed Tuscan butcher Dario Cecchini cutting up a beast before an audience of more than a hundred key people, the heavy hitters of the food industry from around Australasia. Cecchini was joined by Ed Mitchell, a pit master from North Carolina, rockabilly Argentine grill boys Ben Milgate and Elvis Abrahanowicz from Sydney's Porteno, and perhaps the hottest chef in the world that year, US-born Korean chef from New York City David Chang. And I was to emcee. It was a coveted gig and I was lucky enough to have landed it, taking the audience, each paying over $400, on a journey through meat, from butchery to lip-smackingly sticky slices of charcoal-roasted lamb, beef, chicken and pork. But now I had a dirty secret.

The Fire Masterclass was held in a paddock on a bend in the Yarra River embraced by an escarpment that formed a natural amphitheatre. Flood prone, it had never been built on and served for many years as pasture for the milking herd of the nuns living in the Convent of the Good Shepherd just up the hill. Just a few kilometres from the heart of the city, the site was now used by the Collingwood Children's Farm. A safe, protected open space perfect for the slow cooking of scores of animals over fire. The start of the event was delayed due to a few problems with the audiovisual system, and the crowd was growing hot and bothered in the early autumn sun. Eventually the gates swung open and the crowd covered their impatient surge with a meaningful saunter and headed down through the garden and into the paddock, where Ed Mitchell and his son were tending to kilograms of pork slowly roasting in a BBQ as big as a small caravan.

Ushered into the shade of a barn, the crowd was met with great pieces of beef suspended from the rafters by heavy steel chains. A particularly long forequarter was beginning to move ever so slightly in the intermittent breeze.

Dario Cecchini appeared with Melbourne Italian chef Guy Grossi who was to act as translator. Cecchini sorted his knives, the butchery equivalent of clearing one's throat, and then launched into what was a well-honed manifesto of meat.

'Your preoccupation with the tender cuts of meat such as eye fillet coupled with the attitude that "the rest of the carcass is not my problem" needs to be addressed,' he said, chastising the crowd for the Anglosphere's influence of making beef all about steak.

Tuscany's most famous butcher and restaurateur also proved to be a master raconteur. He went on to defend the lesser-loved cuts such as the tail, the shin, the brisket and the head, proclaimed his revulsion at wasting any part of the animal and extolled the beauty of broth—the essence of the beast drawn into a flavoursome liquid that nourishes and consoles. At that point the deputy editor of *Australian Gourmet Traveller*, Pat Nourse, cheekily asked if Cecchini still quoted Dante as he butchered. Taking this as a cue, the butcher, boning knife in hand, approached the forequarter shank, paused, lowered his head and then passionately recited most of Dante Alighieri's *Purgatorio*. For eleven minutes and thirty-four seconds. I was running the event, keeping time and watching the amused audience become bemused. They were happy. Then they went from content to uncomfortable. As he made scant and shallow knife marks in the flesh, he bellowed out his journey into near hell. It was a superb moment of surrealism—what festivals should be—challenging, audacious and out of the ordinary. With the meat now gently swaying in the breeze like a flesh pendulum, he was reaching a climax— trilling his 'r's theatrically as he threw the word *amore* to his beautiful wife. When it comes to awkward public situations, Australians prove to be about as adept as the English—but with suntans. The recital ended and the audience erupted into relieved applause. He quickly boned the shank, spread the marrow inside the meat, seasoned it with salt and a vast quantity of herbs, trussed it with string and baptised it in inordinate amounts of olive oil. More applause. He sent it off to be cooked for three hours.

As the event was running late it was all hands on deck to remove the set for the next chef, Lennox Hastie. He is a Sydney-based chef who was born in the United Kingdom and trained in Michelin-starred restaurants before working with Victor Arguinzoniz at Asador Etxebarri, a charcoal-grill restaurant in the green hills at Atxondo in Spain's Basque Country. There was a quick turnaround from the Italian butcher-cum-raconteur. It fell on me to carry almost my own bodyweight in raw meat onto my shoulders and take it to the coolroom. The thing about properly aged beef is that it smells sweet. The blood has gone and the fresh aromas of slaughter have long dissipated, and what's left is the butteryness of the fat and the stone-like smell of bone. At that moment, in that paddock, on that day I understood I wasn't a vegetarian. I was simply a meat lover who had given up meat. A meat-freegan.

Seeing the beef hanging in the barn earlier that day had transported me back twenty years to a day spent in the Louvre. The shock of recognition in Paris's temple to visual arts had left me punch-drunk. Not just the *Mona Lisa* but Eugène Delacroix's *Liberty Leading the People* and Jacques-Louis David's *The Coronation of Napoleon*. But then, in a dimly lit room, was a large canvas by Rembrandt. Not a portrait or a biblical scene but something secular bordering on profane. It was a painting of a flayed ox. It was an image I had seen many times in our barn on the farm—a quarter of a tonne of meat swinging in the breeze, the internal fat smooth like stone in a limestone cave, the deep red muscles veiled by layers of fat, veins meandering on the surface like red rivers seen from far above. But this was truly and deeply beautiful and painted more than three centuries before.

Once in the coolroom I laid the piece of meat down carefully, all deep yellow fat and greying cut spine, on a cold white shelf. I closed the door, the spring latch sealing it with a confident metallic click behind me.

The day got warmer and the chefs worked hard preparing their dishes. Normally, as emcee, I would act as the audience's proxy and try the food and describe it to them, giving an idea of what the dishes tasted like. But instead I passed the finished dishes to guests and asked them what they could taste, placing the microphone in front of their mouths. A few of them could give precise and clear descriptions of the food. Others fumbled to give language to their experience—for many, food is a one-way relationship that needs no account. I worked the crowd, drawing from them words they might have not thought about using previously. At this point I realised that most people have never been taught how to taste. The general public knows hot, cold, spicy and sweet but after that we are open to anyone's suggestions, making us easy prey for fast food companies who appeal to our base taste instincts. Which makes Australia a nation of gastronomic illiterates. Most people have never been trained how to use their tongue or palate.

It was then David Chang took to a cooking stage in the middle of the paddock. He was demonstrating the Caribbean technique of making jerk chicken, which involves marinating chicken in a thick mixture of vinegar, rum, molasses, ginger, cloves, allspice, nutmeg, chillies and more. At the end of thirty minutes, he passed me his perfectly executed finished dish. Reluctantly, as I wouldn't be getting to New York to taste his food any time soon, I passed the dish to some members of the audience and watched the expressions on their faces change as they tried this incredibly aromatic dish, I assume, for the first time. I watched them sniff at the skin of the chicken, test the texture with their lips, pull the flesh away with their teeth, close their mouths and chew. I could tell from their eyes that Chang's chicken was good. Very good. I could only watch. Thankfully the tasters were front-row food tragics. They understood the process and the way it should taste. They were satisfied and grinned with tacit satisfaction. The audience erupted in applause.

Dario Cecchini was staying in Melbourne for a few more days to take part in the festival and cook a meal with Guy Grossi. The star of the dinner was the beef carcass that hung as the backdrop to Cecchini's butchery demonstration-cum-oratory. When alive it was a massive white Chianina steer, a beast that would tower over most men. Like Cecchini, it was a Tuscan beast, albeit born and raised on a farm in Victoria. Chianina were traditionally bred in the valleys of Tuscany to spend their days as beasts of burden and end them as the famed *bistecca alla Fiorentina* and myriad other dishes. Its predecessors came from Asia sometime during the Bronze Age, making it *Bos indicus*. There is speculation among breeders that its roots lie in an obscure sub-species called *Bos primitiva*. European cattle are *Bos taurus*. This particular animal was raised by a woman who was one of the founding members of Slow Food Melbourne. Australian born to Italian parents, Daniela Mollica had teamed up with her husband,

Sam Walker, soon after they were married to breed these cattle on a coastal farm on the lush Gippsland coast. Together with Grossi and Cecchini, they were hosting the dinner. I had been invited as their guest and there was no vegetarian option. The dinner was a celebration of the beast with fifteen dishes utilising, as Cecchini had extolled, every part of the animal. Declining the hospitality of an Italian is impossible. Declining the hospitality of three: Grossi, Cecchini and Mollica, is a mistake.

I bumped into Mollica a few days before the dinner, at a hotel where a 2-day-long series of food masterclasses was being held. This woman, skilled in Italian and Italian charm, took me aside and very quietly and very politely stated her case as to why the way she raises her beef is ethical. And why I was wrong to give up meat.

'We are not advocates of people eating more beef,' she said. 'That's not the premise on which our company was founded and that is not the message I want to be associated with. I do not think, for many reasons, that eating more beef is healthy. It is not healthy for our bodies and it is not healthy for our planet,' she explained. Her comments were not off the cuff. The argument was well considered, practised and erudite.

'What we believe is that you should eat less meat but better quality meat,' she said. 'Where I think our food system is failing is making meat cheap enough so people can consume it every single day. It moves from something quite important in a nutritional sense to being a volume commodity. That is not the place that meat should be taking in our diet,' she continues. 'When you're seeing steak at a supermarket for $9.95 a kilogram, then meat producers need to bring down the cost of production and hasten the growing period. Which means animals are fed grain in feedlots. And when you go down the grain route you are then forced to look at the philosophical argument about what animals are meant to eat.'

Mollica and Walker at that time killed two animals a month and delivered 10-kilogram boxes of meat to customers' homes for $220. That is $22 a kilogram. Delivered. The boxes contained mostly lesser-loved cuts such as chuck steak and skirt steak that require a modicum of skill to cook. What Daniela was saying to me was that we need to look at the way we consume an entire beautiful animal.

The eye fillet of beef, the muscle that runs along the inside of a cow's spine, and the most desired cut at a wedding function, weighs around 2 kilograms. A steer can weigh over half a tonne, producing a lot of muscle that is not eye fillet, sirloin or T-bone. A steer weighing 600 kilograms, once its head's off, and innards and hide are removed, will weigh around 350 kilograms. Once the bone and fat are removed there is about 270 kilograms of red meat. Our most desired cut is just 2 kilograms. That is crazy.

There are about 28 million head of cattle in Australia with around 9 million slaughtered every year, producing over 2 million tonnes of meat, resulting in around 16 000 tonnes of eye fillet. With 60 per cent of all Australian beef exported, that leaves just under 7000 tonnes of eye fillet to share between 23 million Australians, or roughly half a kilogram each. Every year, on average, we consume individually 33 kilograms of beef and, to complete the statistics, we consume, each year, chicken, pork, lamb, fish, beef and mutton weighing 110 kilograms in total. That's the weight of a footballer. On a daily basis that is 300 grams of animal meat every day. That's a decent steak, a chicken breast from a very large chook, or most of a tin of Spam. Health authorities would be happier if we ate around 100 grams or less of animal flesh a day, with more emphasis on seafood.

With the humiliation dished out to me by the Country Pasty Nazi still taunting my ego; the subterfuge undergone in hiding my new meat-free ways from the food society of Australia; and the most beautiful philosophical dressing-down from one of the most food-informed people in the country, it was time to make some serious, fundamental changes. First, I realised, I would have to learn to cook without meat.

4

Howls of Derisive Laughter

Back in the early 1990s I lived in Edinburgh. My best mate James used to tell me in his clipped Portobello accent: 'In Scotland, we don't have racism. That is because we don't have races.' He would pause to allow the irony to sink in. 'Instead,' he would add with a cheeky grin, 'we have gingers!' This was true. The socially acceptable 'other' in Scotland were people with red hair. Also known as 'gingers'—the first 'g' pronounced hard and the second 'g' pronounced to rhyme with 'singers'. At this point I have a dreadful confession to make. Despite having a ginger-tinted beard, I too took part in the open discrimination against gingers in Scotland. James and I ran a pub quiz that was a demented live game show in which people would publicly humiliate themselves in various Edinburgh pubs in order to gain free drinks. One of the 'games' we played was called 'Ginger Stick'. The stick was simply a long piece of dowel with a carrot dangling from a piece of string tied to the end. One of us would stand on the bar, swinging the carrot over the heads of the packed bar below. The other would press the CD player that had been cued up to the chorus of Ian Dury and the Blockheads' 'Hit Me with Your Rhythm Stick'. You know how it goes—Dury, in his gruff London accent, asks repeatedly to be hit with a rhythm stick. The pub regulars, mostly university students, knew what was coming and would shout along with the chorus. At the tops of their voices they would demand to be hit with the rhythm stick and shout out three times, 'HIT ME'.

The stick was allegedly imbued with special powers that enabled it to detect the 'most ginger' person in the bar. As it swung around, the strawberry blondes and other slightly ginger-haired people would self-consciously try to avoid being under the carrot lest it tarry above their mop. Inevitably it danced ceremoniously above the reddest head in the pub and that poor person would be dragged up onto the bar, and submitted to some humiliating questions and forced to explain their gingerness to the room in a kind of twisted Lothian Inquisition. There was a lot of sympathetic laughter and they were given a voucher for a pint (£1 back then) and then sent back to drink it with their chums.

Cruelly, the Ginger Stick would then spring back to life if there was a person in the bar with dyed red hair, be it a pleasant henna tint or a more antisocial punk red. Ian Dury would arc up again and that person would be dragged up onto the bar and forced to explain why they chose, of all things, to have red hair. For further humiliation they were given some tat we had bought from the op shop—perhaps a *Blue Peter* yearbook, an album of Scottish laments or just a tartan lampshade. For the drunken Scottish crowd, a natural-born ginger person was the focus of mild derision. When a person who had made the choice to be different was pointed out, the tone of the room changed noticeably. People don't like other people who choose to be different. I learned that when it comes to discrimination, there is safety in numbers.

THE LETTER

When I started this experiment I was prepared for a lot of things to change in my life. I was expecting my weight to change, my food bill to drop and my cholesterol level to lower. What I wasn't prepared for was the backlash. The day after the story about going meat-free ran in the *Good Living* section, as it was known then, of *The Sydney Morning Herald*, I received this email from a person working with Meat and Livestock Australia.

Dear Richard,

I read your piece in *Good Living* yesterday. Wow what a change! Great news about losing the six kilos too—congratulations. Perhaps it was the lack of processed meat such as jamon and bacon rather than lean beef, lamb or goat which contributed to your weight loss?

You mentioned also concerns about animal welfare and the environmental impact of animal farming in your article—is it possible for you to give me a little more detail about your concerns with regards to the farming of beef, lamb and goat; I'd be really interested in hearing about them and understanding if there is anything the industry can do to allay them.

Have you decided yet if you're going to keep it up?

Yours,

xxxxxxxxxx

What I learned from that day on is that there are a lot of people in the world who don't like vegetarians. Announcing to the world that you have given up meat means people say things to your face they wouldn't normally say. The above email had a derisive tone regarding me eating a lot of bacon and jamón and assumed I didn't eat lean meat. That someone in the meat industry would want to assuage my concerns about animal welfare is like Clive Palmer talking down the dangers of coaldust. It was not the voice one would be addressed with normally. There was a noticeable shift in the dynamic. Usually someone from an industry body contacting a food journalist would use very professional language. This was very personal and bordered on the dismissive. Something had changed. It was something I had to get used to.

DERISION

'Why aren't you eating meat?' asked a chef mate. 'Was it on doctor's orders?' That's Michael Zandegu speaking. He's a hardworking chef who has cooked for big names, and now makes some really simple and tasty little dishes at the farmers' markets where we shop. He goes around all the stallholders very early in the morning and buys from them the least attractive fruit and veg. While it is still dark he wanders over to

Aphrodite, the organic market gardener, and picks over her beetroots, finding the more misshapen ones, the beetroot most likely to be left on the shelf at the end of the day. He drops by the other farmers and seeks out the deformed carrots that look like a rude and amusing appendage. He buys the cabbages that may have just a little too much slug damage to make them appealing even to the most ethical cook and he brings them back to his makeshift kitchen in a corner of the market. For the next hour he uses his impeccable knife skills to slice, dice and julienne the lumpen produce into salads that are metabolically and gastronomically good. On this day, his set-up was perched next to Warialda Belted Galloway. This is the name of the award-winning beef sold at farmers' markets. Zandegu was cooking some of their lesser-loved cuts of meat from their mobile butcher's shop that does the rounds of the markets. He'd stuff a fresh bread roll with some juicy pieces of grilled intercostal—the muscles that run between the rib bones—and top with a great serve of chopped salad. I had always ordered a roll without the meat from him, long before I gave up meat, for, like most people, I have never been able to stomach fat-marble-score-five beef before lunchtime.

Apart from bacon, I had never considered meat a breakfast food. But my having announced I was no longer eating meat allowed him to openly deride me. His market neighbours, Lizette and Allen, with whom I had previously enjoyed a very genial relationship, called out to me across the heads of their customers. 'What's wrong with you? Gone soft. Bloody vegetarian!' It was meant to be fun, but when people team up against you it oversteps the line.

OUTSiDER

It was a Sunday afternoon, at a late BBQ lunch. Middle-aged men in loud shirts stared transfixed at the grill plate as the alpha male with the tongs turned the meat. When men of means get to a certain age they become picky with their meat. No longer able to consume large amounts of animal fats without impunity, they choose small amounts of premium product. The same goes for wine. Single vineyard, single block, late harvest, basket pressed, open ferment, unfiltered and aged in old oak. Over forty and you consume less but it's of the best. Jack Daniel's? No. You'll go for a Tasmanian Highland rye whisky made from farm-grown grain distilled in a hand-beaten copper still. On the grill were Wessex Saddleback sausages and dry-aged sirloins. By this stage I had pretty much perfected the lentil burger (see page 179 for recipe). I placed them on the grill beside the cooking meat. My host reeled. 'What are they?' he said. 'Lentil burgers,' I replied. 'Get them off!' he demanded.

It was as if the lentil burgers were contaminated with something that would make the meat impure, like they were impregnated with some bacteria that would destroy the wholesome meatiness of the steak. 'No animals died in the making of these burgers,' I joked. But he wasn't joking. The host took the tongs off me and moved the lentil burgers to the perimeter of the grill—the part where the burner underneath had failed and there was no heat. I had to wait until the steak and sausages had been cooked before I had space to cook the burgers. The meat was removed and the 'carnivores', as they chose to call themselves, moved to the cool of the inside kitchen. I was left outside to turn my burgers. Being vegetarian puts you on the outer, literally.

At the table someone cracked a gag about vegetarians. 'What do Aborigines call vegetarians?' There was an appropriate comedic pause. 'Bad hunters.' Laughter ensued. Someone else chipped in. 'Did you hear about the vegan devil worshipper?' they asked rhetorically. 'He sold his soul to seitan!' Boom boom.

IT'S THEIR FAULT

'How many wines by the glass?' I asked the restaurant owner. I was doing a piece for the newspaper and it's a standard question a food writer asks restaurant owners to get a snapshot of their beverage offer. I was in a regional pub brewery with a restaurant. The owner was a 50-plus woman who had a sweet hardness that successful women in pubs either have or adopt. 'What are the bestselling mains on the menu?' I asked. 'We have a really good relationship with the local butcher, who has some good grass-fed beef,' she said. 'So we are known for our steaks. And perhaps the best chicken parma in the district,' she added. This is a usual boast and a good indication of not only where owners rank themselves in the local dining pantheon but where the profit centres of the menu may lie. 'The chef hand-beats out the chicken breasts and crumbs them with house-baked breadcrumbs. It's really good.' She enthusiastically also talked up the beef pie, pasta with pork ragout, a Moroccan lamb dish and pizza with prosciutto.

'And how many vegetarian options?' I asked. This is also a standard question. It reflects just how much the chef has embraced vegetables in their cooking, as well as their overall attitude to hospitality. If you find yourself in the disabled toilet in a restaurant or hotel, for example, and you can't move for mops and boxes of toilet paper, then you have a fair idea about the manager's attitude to accessibility.

When I asked the owner about the vegetarian options you could almost hear her eyes rolling around her head. 'We can do a risotto for them,' she said, dropping her words like she was trying to shake something wet from her hands.

'Anything else?' I asked.

'No,' she said curtly, watching me take notes. 'Well, it's their own fault!' she added.

I didn't make a comment. I took some photos of the rather good beer and left. But consider that change in language: 'It's their fault'. Pull this apart and repack it in a manner that explains the underpinning philosophy and thought and you get something like this: 'Well, we go to a lot of trouble sourcing and making the meals we like eating ourselves, which are based around 50 per cent animal protein by mass on the plate. But when it comes to cooking food that doesn't involve meat, we are not that enthused. To tell you the truth, we resent people not eating meat. They're not trying to fit in. They are making extra work for us and for themselves. So we prefer to dissuade them because, after all, it's their fault.'

THE CHEFS WHO GET IT

One of my favourite old cookbooks is *New Standard Cookery* published by Odhams Press Ltd, London, in 1933. The one I have must be the Australian edition, for it has an 'Australian Kitchen' chapter that has such classic dishes as Illawarra mushroom pie and stuffed baked pawpaw (or pumpkin), a recipe for both stewed and creamed bandicoot, and a roasting method for black swan, bush turkey, wallaby and Mallee hen. (The Mallee hen, or Malleefowl, is a large, mostly ground-dwelling bird that lives, as the name suggests, in the Mallee and is now listed as a threatened species). The book is out of date and out of print. It may have been out of touch, listing recipes such as Tasmanian pineapple whip, based, of course, on the great pineapple plantations of the subtropical Derwent Valley.

The book suggests that meat 'is the substantial course of the dinner, and many people would not consider the meal complete without it'. Over eighty years later the thinking in many restaurant kitchens has not changed.

There is a cooking gag that goes something along these lines: Diner to top chef: What do you have for vegetarians? Top chef to diner: Contempt.

Dining out by a person who does not eat meat is often made easy by the absence of any choice at all. The dated dining model of a bistro-style menu generally works on five or more choices in entree, main and dessert. There is generally a 'vegetarian option' in the entree and the main. When a waiter describes the menu, the words are loaded with coded intonation. 'Vegetarian OPTION' is pronounced like a game-show voice-over man describing the consolation prize. As in 'Thanks, Jim, sorry you didn't do so well tonight but Jo has something for you.' And 'Never mind, Jim. You don't go home empty-handed. There's the board game from Crown and Andrews, the stickpin from Germani, plus our very own "vegetarian option".' The vegetarian option is generally a pasta or risotto dish, the kitchen logic being that customers need to walk out the door feeling full. If they won't get full from animal protein they can get it from starch. And dairy.

Melbourne chef Matt Wilkinson famously declared that when it comes to knowing where food comes from and what is seasonal and fresh, most Australian chefs were 'lazy and ignorant'. Wilkinson got a lot of flak for his vehement views. Other chefs took to social media to tell him to shut his mouth. I applauded his bravado and mocked up a range of kitchen wear, which included a poorly photoshopped image of Matt wearing an apron with the words 'lazy and ignorant' scribbled in with digital ink. Wilkinson laughed. I agreed with his sentiments. Chefs who know where food comes from are in the minority. In many kitchens you will find a list of suppliers: butcher, seafood, fruit and veg, dry goods, frozen goods. Sometimes the list is that short. Go into Matt's kitchen and he'll be on the phone to his pork supplier, consoling them about the lack of rain, or, the wild-dog attack on their free-range herd. Chefs like Matt go to farms on their days off and holidays, to learn about food, how it is grown, when it is at its seasonal best and how they can manage their kitchen around the supply. Another really good cook is Stefano de Pieri, cooking in Mildura on the Murray. He prepares a degustation-only menu that changes daily to take into account what comes in to his kitchen each day. A lot of the food is grown by his local mates in their small gardens. I don't think Stefano would know how to prepare the frozen goods from a food-service truck if one hit him.

The best Australian chefs are hardworking and hungry for knowledge. They know meat is a shortcut to yumminess. But to produce really good vegetarian food at a high standard demands chefs have a good knowledge of food and an understanding of how flavour works. This involves a broad range of skills and understanding of ingredients from a range of cultures. These were key lessons I was to learn regarding my own kitchen. I don't come from a culture that celebrates meatless meals. Meat is a celebration in itself. I had to cherrypick from cultures that don't have meat at the centre of the meal.

Unburdened from the shackles of expecting that a meal contain meat, I was free to explore the extraneous sections of menus. And this is where, I discovered, good chefs are at their best. Raymond Capaldi is a Scots-born chef who grew up in Prestonpans, on the outskirts of Edinburgh. When I lived there I was told it wasn't a place one visited unless one intended to score class-A drugs. Capaldi is known as much for his colourful tongue as he is his rich brogue. What outshines both is his ability to cook. He is sensational. Perhaps the best soup I have ever had is his butternut pumpkin soup. 'You get butternut pumpkin,' he told me. 'You cook it in fuckin' goat's milk. You fuckin' season it. You put it in the fuckin' Thermomix. You serve it. Fuckin' delicious.' At his now-closed Melbourne CBD restaurant Hare & Grace he served an inspired dish of mock pasta to appease the gluten-free crowd from the surrounding business towers. He took thick rings of onion, cut them so they formed broad fettuccini-width strips and blanched them to soften them and remove the sharp tang of onion. He dressed the hot onion 'fettuccini' in cream and egg, seasoned with a little cayenne, which thickened when it hit the hot onion, to form a sauce. He called the dish 'low carbonara'. It was fuckin' delicious.

Another chef of note is Riccardo Momesso. Momesso is a natural-born killer. He is never happier than when he has a shotgun to his shoulder, blowing small birds out of the sky. Now a restaurateur, he combined his love of hunting with his skill at cooking traditional Italian food by sneaking some of his wild game into the ragout and sausages when he was working with the team at Sarti. This is a modern Italian restaurant in the east end of Melbourne. The notes I made from just one meal list wild mushroom and *caprino suppli*—beautiful golden bullet-shaped croquettes of rice flecked and flavoured with pieces of pine mushroom and porcini, with the clean finish and lactic tang of *caprino* (soft goat's milk cheese). There was also baked artichoke with pieces of crisp almond and soft buffalo mozzarella. And a masterpiece in umami—pasta *al farro* with eggplant, tomato, slow-cooked Spanish onion and pecorino. The low, slow braise of the vegetables reduced them to a sweet and savoury, but thick and delicious, sauce that clung to the pasta, handmade spirals rolled tight around a wooden skewer. Bringing it together, like a culinary von Karajan, was the deft addition of salty pecorino cheese. Amazing flavour and without any mention that the meal was vegetarian.

As Matt Wilkinson explained to me:

> Chefs use animal protein as a crutch. They will finish a meat dish with jus, which is basically super-concentrated broken-down protein (amino acid). It tastes very, very nice and is all very yummy. But try to get most chefs to be able to deliver that amount of flavour on the plate without using meat and they won't be able to. Why? It is because they either were not trained properly or are too arrogant to embrace the truth that the best cooking reflects a deep understanding of *all* ingredients, including, of course, vegetables. Vegetables should be the cornerstone of every meal. I would like to have a restaurant with a menu where meat doesn't feature. It is part of the dish but it is used as just another ingredient. My biggest fear would not be that the staff and customers wouldn't take kindly to it but that I would be labelled a vegetarian chef. Or a meat-free chef. Getting past the lazy thinking of general consensus is very hard.

Wilkinson went on to write *Mr Wilkinson's Favourite Vegetables* and *Mr Wilkinson's Simply Dressed Salads*, books that have sold over 100 000 copies worldwide. There is a lesson in that for resistant chefs. Wilkinson is way ahead of the pack when it comes to thinking about food and is always a good soul to bounce ideas off.

Another chef who is never frightened of letting vegetables do a solo act is French-born Nicolas Poelaert. Almost as a swan song, in his own restaurant Embrasse, he produced a 6-course vegan meal, in concert with Tomato social media head Ed Charles, that didn't use any animal products. This was in September 2011. Anyone who has tried to grow veg in Victoria knows that September is the leanest month of the year. It is right at the end of winter and the spring flush is yet to begin.

The evening started with some smoked bread, a portion of grassy and fruity Mount Zero biodynamic olive oil piped inside. Then there was a dish of pumpkin, bergamot, Meyer lemon and horseradish. He was able to send out a dish that you would have sworn was fish, it was so redolent of the sea, but was in fact made with broccoli, brussels sprouts, grilled zucchini, sugar beet, warrigal greens and seagrass juice.

'Vegetables play an important role in Embrasse's kitchen and fill more room on the plate than is generally the case in other gourmet restaurants,' wrote Poelaert at the time. Nowhere on the menu of that truly memorable meal was the word vegan used.

Then there was the degustation at Jacques Reymond, a dozen courses of modern French cooking prepared with Zen-like elegance and no fish or flesh. It was a year later and the French-born chef was at the height of his powers, with an exit strategy in the back of his mind. Just over six months later, he announced he was retiring from three chef's hat fine dining.

One outstanding dish was a simple terrine of potatoes layered with Beauforte cheese. This is a French cow's milk cheese that is smear-ripened with a mixture of salt and salt-loving cultures and left to mature. When warm, it sings of the high altitude pastures on which the dairy herds grazed. Reymond and his team finished the dish by slicing the terrine and searing it in a pan, adding a glazed savoury caramel crust to the cheese and potatoes. It was an understated triumph exhibiting a lifetime of understanding. It was simple and delicious. He extracted the maximum possible amount of flavour from that dish. There were the natural savoury elements from the cheese that were highlighted by the deft use of what is known as the Maillard reaction. This is when starch and amino acid recombine at high temperature to create new compounds with darker colours, more savoury flavours and a lovely bittersweet balance. Think skin on roast lamb, or the very outside of a crust of dark sourdough.

To understand why Reymond knows how to cook food so well, it helps to understand where he came from. He was raised in the small town of Cuiseaux in Jura, France. His house was above a mill where his grandfather milled walnuts and hazelnuts for oil. In Reymond's words:

> I was brought up in a stone house in the village where, under the house, there was a huge stone driven by a donkey going around and around, crushing the nuts in season. We grew up with black hands peeling the walnuts. The first extraction of the oil was pure perfection. Then my grandfather pressed the ground nuts. The second extraction. Then he had a small wood fire and he would take the pressed nuts—imagine something similar to the plug of coffee you have in an espresso machine—and he would gently roast these, engulfing the village and the villages for five kilometres in the aroma of wood smoke, walnuts and hazelnuts. After the oil was pressed from these we went fishing in the river, with the roasted nuts to use as bait. Nothing was wasted.

Reymond grew up with the aroma of nut oil filling the house each autumn. His grandfather was also the regional rabbit butcher. He went from village to village, preparing the rabbits according to the wants of the housewives. When Reymond was young he showed enough interest in his grandfather's trade for the older man to take him aside, telling him, 'Jacques, you are an interesting young man, you show talent and observance'. Reymond's grandfather left him the leather bag of knives he used when butchering the local rabbits. Reymond was, decades later, painted with that bag for the Archibald Prize.

Reymond trained at the 3-Michelin-star restaurant L'Oustau de Baumanière in Provence, and the restaurant at Hotel La Verniaz at Evian, near Geneva. He became deeply proficient and knowledgeable not only about his native French food but about Asian ingredients. This knowledge was gained by working in the Amazon and the north-east of Brazil, with the descendants of black slaves who used ingredients such as ginger and kaffir lime leaves in their culinary vernacular. It was here that he decided to work these ingredients into his personal cuisine. He returned to France and opened his own restaurant in Cuiseaux, obtaining a Michelin star.

'But I was frustrated that I couldn't get those fresh exotic ingredients,' he told me in a later discussion, after the degustation event.

This was the impetus to move to Australia—a place where the exotic Asian ingredients were easier to come by. When he arrived in 1983 he worked with Mietta O'Donnell at her eponymous restaurant. He opened his first restaurant in 1986 and his mansion-based restaurant in 1992. He remained true to his classic French training and cooked according to the seasons. But he had given himself permission to employ the other influences that informed him, as he cooked the light, thoughtful and considered dishes he became known for. He never veered towards fusion, instead simply creating a cuisine that was a generous and playful extrapolation of nouvelle cuisine.

'I let product express itself and only add other ingredients to complement the flavour,' said Reymond, his eyes lighting up at the mere mention of vegetables. 'There should only be three or four ingredients in a dish. It is about understanding and respecting the ingredient. With vegetables, some need a good kick, some need some acidity, some will need some element of fat, such as the grandfather's oils [walnut or hazelnut]. Then there is the cooking technique—roasted, steamed, braised, or wrapped in paperbark or silicon paper. Sometimes you want to concentrate the flavours, such as cooking the celeriac in a salt crust.' When he said this he puckered his lips as he remembered the flavour and texture. 'This is such a wonderful way of cooking celeriac. Outside is a thick, almost impenetrable crust but inside the flesh is soft and intense and delicious,' he said. But, focusing, he hammered home his point. 'It is essential to understand vegetables much more than meat or fish because of the water content of the vegetable,' he said. 'Because you have to extract the water without killing the flavour of the ingredient. That is where you have to understand each vegetable. You have to draw out the moisture to concentrate the flavour and you have to find the right cooking technique to do this without killing the very essence of the vegetable you are trying to highlight. It is a very fine balancing act but it is not difficult to understand. It just takes time.'

One of the other great dishes Reymond prepared in that degustation was a simple tempura with enoki mushrooms, matched with a bright and lively young sage and stinging nettle puree, a little segment of poached nectarine and some granules of fresh wasabi. It was stunning.

Thankfully there is a turnaround in the attitude chefs have towards vegetables. This will only increase as animal protein becomes more expensive. The price of beef has increased by 20 per cent and the price of popular cuts of pork by 25 per cent in the few months leading up to the end of 2015 alone. I watched this economic effect on the kitchen of a chef near Madrid, Fernando del Cerro from Casa José in Aranjuez. He has a restaurant near the market in the old summer capital of Spain. I dined there in September 2008 and then six months after the GFC first hit. His menu had changed from whole fish on the bone and great prime cuts of pork to vegetable braises and much smaller portions of lesser-loved cuts of meat. He dropped his costs, dropped his price but kept his profit margin. He is a chef who knows how to cook and knows how to cook vegetables. He is lucky. He works with some of the best growers in the country. He is still in business while many others in the top end of the industry have closed their doors.

For some time the relationship between chef, or cook, and grower has been truncated and tenuous. Most chefs don't know where their food comes from. There has been no feedback loop for cooks and chefs to get growers to raise the bar, and no way the growers can educate those in the kitchen about the way fruit and veg change with the season. In the last decade and a half we have seen the rise of farmers' markets, where real farmers drive to the towns and cities to sell what they picked from their farm the day before. There is also the neo-peasant arm of the hipster movement that sees young people return to the land or take up farming. While this might not be sustainable in the long run, with many young couples deep in debt with shallow returns, it is in the short term providing some really excellent quality produce to the food system.

It is an appealing option to many. Former Longrain chef Marty Boetz gave up a dazzling career in a popular Sydney restaurant to become a farmer. He's a good example of the new dialogue that is happening between chefs and their growers. Out on the fertile flats of the Hawkesbury River he grows quite sensational vegetables on his farm, Cooks Co-op. Picked each morning, they are hand-delivered to restaurants by his team. Beautiful greens, marrows, tomatoes, beans. He knows what chefs want and has taught himself how to grow it accordingly. It's a 2-way street: he can also offer ideas on how to prepare more novel veg.

I thought I would learn something by giving up meat. I didn't realise it would re-educate me. The unintended consequence was that I was learning something really important every single time I went to talk to someone about what I was doing. Those with good brains and the ability to think outside the dominant paradigm were downloading all this invaluable information and experience. Something clicked: I realised I was on the gastronomic equivalent of the Camino de Santiago. A slow-paced period of reflection, abstinence, penance, perhaps, and unexpected commitment, with the possibility of an epiphany. I knew this was no longer just research for a newspaper article. So hungry, no—greedy for knowledge I redoubled my efforts, extended the period of abstinence twelvefold and embarked on this book you hold in your hands.

5

Loaded Language against Lentils

'So, Richard. Where are you getting your protein from,' quizzed Stephanie. The doyenne of Australian cookery, Stephanie Alexander, like Kylie, Bert and other great Australians, is now known only by her first name. She eyed me up and down. 'If you're not eating meat, you have to be getting your protein from somewhere else,' she said, challenging my openly meat-free lifestyle. Here was a woman whom I respect greatly grilling me in front of a small audience at a function at the State Library Victoria. Stern, and maintaining her authorial tone, I felt that she was not only questioning the very premise on which I was basing my experiment, but also my knowledge of human nutrition that would give me the authority to talk publicly on this matter. I patted my belly—I am in no way a small man—and assured her that I was surviving quite well on my new-found repertoire of dishes based on different coloured vegetables, grains, legumes and fungus. Not only had I been trawling the streets for dishes I could learn from the local Vietnamese, Lebanese and Sudanese restaurants, I had also dusted off cookbooks in the Cornish library. I worked up recipes from books on my shelves that I had bought but never opened. I returned to the classics: English writer Elizabeth David, who championed the food of France and the Mediterranean; Madhur Jaffrey and her recipes from the Subcontinent; Marcella Hazan, who wrote beautifully of the food of Italy. I even referred to the doyenne herself, and opened up Stephanie's *Kitchen Garden Companion* and cooked from that. The author in front of me pursed her lips and then broke into a cheeky smile to assure me that this was just a friendly goading.

I didn't go to the library unprepared. I knew where to look. I had been advised by a nutritionist, who had educated me on what foods to put together to get a really balanced diet. 'Tell me exactly what you are eating,' said Catherine Saxelby. She is a well-known nutritionist who I had worked with on stories before. I trusted her judgement. Previously I had always been suspicious of the nutritionists who had once recommended aspartame and margarine.

I like her because she doesn't take a reductionist view of food. A reductionist nutritionist is one who only sees food as the sum of its most basic constituent molecules. It's a stream of thinking that divorces food from its interlaced cultural, social, gastronomic and sensory contexts, and sees it as something that is broken down in the great vat-like mix of acids and enzymes of our digestive tract, distilled into useful, or otherwise, compounds, to fuel the human machine. The reductionist nutritionist is the equivalent of an art critic who describes a painting as a canvas adequately covered in an array of different paints.

'Not a dead creature has passed my lips for several months,' I explained to Catherine. 'Except perhaps some weevils.' These I had found in a packet of lentils after I had cooked and eaten a dhal made with them. I told her that I was still eating a small amount of cheese and a few eggs. 'Okay, I just wanted to make sure whether you were vegan or not,' she said. 'Because vegan diets are a little harder to balance.' She quizzed me on the food I was eating, making sure that I was preparing food made from whole grains such as brown rice and barley, and giving a tick to the renaissance of quinoa, freekeh (smoked cracked wheat) and faro. 'Whole grains plus legumes, such as chickpeas, lentils and beans, plus the small amount of cheese and eggs, will look after your protein,' she explained. 'But there are a lot of nutrients in meat and fish that are more difficult to get from a vegetarian diet. What you may run short of are iron and zinc.' Iron is found in whole grains and leafy greens but the iron is not readily available to the body; it is more accessible when eaten with vitamin C—a lemon-juice-based dressing, she explained, is perfect. Zinc, which is responsible for our immunity and sense of smell, is best absorbed from seafood such as oysters, red meat and chicken. It is also found in grains and vegetables. 'Vitamin B12, essential for the prevention of anaemia, is basically found in red meat and some in eggs,' said Catherine, 'although there is evidence that mushrooms can provide vitamin B12.' She also suggested a diet rich in flax seed, walnuts or pecan nuts for plant-based omega-3.

'You're a 44-year-old man,' she said. 'You'll be fine. But if you were a young growing teenager, or were a woman, particularly a pregnant woman, I'd be watching you a lot more carefully. Anyone taking on a vegetarian or vegan diet should consult an accredited dietitian to make sure they are eating well and widely from the range of food available.' I silently thanked her for not mentioning supplements in plastic-capped bottles. The concept that nutritional food can be broken down and isolated into its key components and concentrated into a pill is a bizarre confluence of industry and science fiction. 'Good luck and watch out for bacon!' she said in high spirits that barely concealed an underlying serious tone. 'Cured pig flesh is the one thing that unsticks so many people trying to give up meat because it has such an enticing aroma.'

With those words of warning ringing in my ears I turned my attention to understanding the concept of protein. It had been two months since I had gone meat-free and I felt that I didn't really understand many of the basics of what food contains what nutrition, and which nutrition does what in the human body.

Proteins are building blocks in the human body. They make up our muscles, skin, hair, eyes, organs and toenails. Protein itself is made up of amino acids joined together with other bits and pieces. Protein is like a chunk of preassembled Lego blocks that is made up of loads of little interlinked blocks of amino acids that the body pulls apart and rearranges according to need. When we eat, the protein in food is deconstructed into its constituent amino acids by the enzymes and chemicals in our digestive system. Our body then reassembles these amino acids into all sorts of new proteins that form our very beings. Pinch yourself. Pinch yourself hard. Everything you feel from the skin between your fingers to the pain itself involves protein.

Nutritionists divide the amino acids that make up protein into two different kinds: essential and non-essential. Essential amino acids are histidine, leucine, isoleucine, valine, lysine, threonine, tryptophan, methionine and phenylalanine. Which sound more like animo superheroes than compounds essential for the healthy functioning of the adult human body. These are found together in what nutritionists have traditionally referred to as a 'complete protein'. It is interesting to note that there are other amino acids the human body requires to survive, but we have found a way of synthesising these ourselves in our own bodies. Until recently the message was to eat complete proteins daily. This thinking continues, with health and diet manuals turning over the same instructions to eat red meat, poultry, seafood, eggs and dairy products, as they contain complete protein.

Most vegetables, however, don't contain all the essential amino acids. There are global culinary traditions that have cleverly overcome this. The town of Atlixco is a fine example; it sits under the shadow of Popocatépetl, an active volcano in Central Mexico. It is always growling and sending off puffs of smoke, threatening to erupt. Which gives the locals a fatalistic attitude to life and a dark sense of humour—a local baker bakes conical buns finished with white sugar at the apex, as a replica of Popocatépetl. As if, somehow, by making an effigy of the snow-capped summit it would stay that way and not be suddenly melted by a surge of hot gas and lava blasting from the bowels of the earth. There has been a market in the town since long before the conquistadors arrived in Mexico. Five hundred or so years later and not much has changed. Instead of woven palm mats, market-stall holders now lay out blue plastic tarpaulin on which they display the piles of black, red, yellow and brown beans they sell. I had visited the area shortly before researching and shooting photographs for a book on Mexican food. In the heart of the market was a middle-aged couple who tended to their piles of different coloured beans. She would rake them every now and then to keep their pyramid shape but also to create some colour and movement to attract the shoppers. One lot of beans was pinkish brown with mottled dark-brown marks on its skin. These were called *frijoles culebra* or snake beans. They had been bred sometime in the distant past to be planted alongside corn seeds. As the corn grew and unfurled its long broad leaves, the bean shoots would follow, snaking a leading tendril around the stalk as they grew together skyward. Harvested and dried together, they were both stored for eating throughout the year. If the Mexicans had grown and eaten just one without the other, they would have had an incomplete diet, unless they went out hunting for wildfowl, fish or small deer. Most beans are deficient in methionine, while corn lacks lysine and tryptophan. Together the corn and grain formed the binary food foundation for much of the diet of Mesoamericans, complemented by squash and tomatoes from the garden, and wild herbs, or *quiletes*, from the surrounding woods. The Mesoamericans also discovered that if dried corn is soaked in water, with a little lime added, the proteins in the corn bind together to form a dough. The process is called nixtamalisation. Without nixtamalisation we would never have had tacos. An added benefit is the release of available niacin, a B-group vitamin that staves off the dietary disease of pellagra. On this diet the Aztecs created shining cities of pyramids and floating farms that awed the Spaniards.

Many empires have been built on pulses and grains. Roman centurions marched on porridges of barley and fava beans. The power of the maharajah was based on armies marching on lentils and rice. The Chinese emperors led armies fed on fermented soy and rice. The grain and legume dietary duo is mirrored in Europe, where broad beans and barley are sown together.

What is interesting is the underlying bias in contemporary nutritional literature towards meat, describing it as 'complete'. The implication being that most vegetables are 'incomplete', from which the obvious inference is made that vegetables are inferior. It's logically correct but words have more than one meaning. Seventy per cent of the protein in the Western diet comes from animal protein. In the rest of the world more than 60 per cent of the population's protein comes from vegetable protein. In the reductionist world of nutritional numbers and statistics, a steak is supreme and lentils lesser. Figures like these, however, don't take into account the concept of culture. In traditional diets where meat is scarce or not eaten for cultural reasons, cuisines have developed that combine legumes with whole grains and vegetables. Indians eat lentils. Yes. But in a meal that most likely will also contain rice, wheat, cheese or yoghurt, and other vegetables. Mexicans eat corn. Yes. In the form of tortillas, filled with cooked beans, cheese and perhaps foraged wild greens.

In the protein argument against the vegetarian diet, it is steak versus vegetables. Steak will always win in this loaded game. It's a simple concept and easy to comprehend. It underpins much of the understanding of the vegetarian diet and informs a lot of the bias and prejudice against vegetarians. It's like pitting Tom Jones in an eisteddfod against Art Garfunkel. Meaty old Tom is always going to win against reedy little Garfunkel. But combine Art with his naturally occurring companion Paul Simon and you create a completely different beast with amazing range, complexity and nuance. Arguments hate complexity, so it's rare the meat-versus-veg-protein argument pits lean beef against corn tortillas with refried beans, or lamb chops take on spiced dhal and rice. It's usually just one lump of animal versus one lump of vegetable. The language we use to describe food does not make for a fair fight.

6

Meat Map

I was now in the market for a new type of food experience. In my previous life as a committed carnivore I had a meat map of Melbourne and Victoria seared into the navigational sector of my brain. I knew where the best meat was to be had and for a variety of reasons. There was Cut Price Tony. Not that his meat was cheap, but his face was so brutal it always seemed that his meat would have to be cheap. An old-fashioned Italian butcher who butted his fags into the pools of serum out the back of the inner-city butcher's shop where he made the best fennel and garlic sausages in town, the ones the Italian migrants bought before they began making their own sausages from their own pigs. Then there was Werner. Swiss and cheeky, he was a butcher who was so charming he had the middle-class matrons eating wieners out of the palm of his hand. With his flashing smile he would entice the wife standing at your side into his aura of Teutonic smallgoods, right there in front of you. His bratwurst and weisswurst were the best in town. For good lamb I had to wait for the deliveryman. He would bring a plain cardboard box, into which Jenny Anderson, a fifth-generation farmer from Ned Kelly country, had neatly packed one of her own sweet little lambs, to the front door. When my daughters were born she sneaked lambskins into the box for them to sleep on. Then there was the best steak in Australia. It is grown by an ex-butcher called Bones. He owns a pub and a farm. His mum owns a butcher's shop, and his brother, the abattoirs. His cattle are grass fed on native pastures and are sent just a few kilometres to slaughter. They are hung for twenty-four days, if not longer, and Bones would save the best cuts for his mates. It was worth the half-day drive, or waiting until racing season when he arrived trackside for a week, the boot of his sedan packed with homegrown, grass-fed, dry-aged Hereford steaks. I remember once receiving a late-night delivery of one of his specials—spring lambs grazing on native pasture that had gone to seed, giving protein-rich pasture to the lambs. It was in a supermarket car park. The lamb had been dressed but not butchered. This meant that it was dead, beheaded, dehooved, skun, eviscerated and chilled. Not words one uses every day at the office. It was sitting on a blanket without a cover in the back seat of his sedan; it was a hot day and the aircon inside was keeping it cool. He pulled it out and threw it over his shoulder. Judging by the astonished reactions of the other people in the car park, not many were happy to see a whole dead lamb.

Those days have passed now. I had to make a new map in my mind.

SOUL MAN

The first time I walked into Soulfood Café was the second-last time. The bare-wood interior of the inner-Melbourne café was indicative of the vegetarian ethos of the restaurant. It was unadorned, down-market in a back-to-the-earth kind of way. So was the Friday-night crowd. This vegetarian restaurant had been a Fitzroy stalwart since the junkies were roaming free in this once-unloved Victorian-era strip of Smith Street. The dealers and their clients would disguise their deals with a lateral handslap. The passing of a little bag of white powder—part heroin, part glucose, part horse dope—was obfuscated by the mock-streetwise gesture. Many of the diners of Soulfood were young urban professionals, slightly pale for that time of the year and slightly serious for that time of the week. They were interlaced with groups with badly kept hair, colourful clothing and scant footwear, and surrounded by the fading aroma of sandalwood. The menu was big and inviting but was reminiscent of meals in share houses when the resident vegetarian was throwing a dinner party: tofu wrapped in roti, 'pumpkinopita', chickpea curry. The food was good, including the rich chickpea stew with evenly cut vegetables and fresh spices lacing the sauce. The literature around the room was preaching to the converted, with calls to political rallies and notices about spiritual enlightenment classes. There was a certain aura of self-aware spiritual superiority. Having never paid too much attention to vegetarian aesthetics or culture before, it was taking me a while to absorb it all.

I stepped out into the early evening and could smell meat in the air. While well-intentioned young couples hovered prevaricatingly outside the windows of the vego place, pondering about committing to lentils that night, the newly opened hipster burger place a little way down and across the street was heaving with bearded young men and freshly tattooed women making their way through burgers and fries, and longnecks of Melbourne Bitter beer.

A few weeks later I walked down Smith Street again. My partner had opened a clothing store just around the corner, in Gertrude Street. I walked into a glorious old bank that had been turned into a hipster gift shop. I couldn't help but notice the inordinate number of meat-orientated gifts, such as bacon bandaids and meat moustaches. It had been a few short years since the rise of hipsterism as a cultural force had seen the blending of anti-fashion as fashion, lowbrow as highbrow, and sheer force of online numbers had made it the dominant trend. I had been to Los Angeles for work eighteen months earlier and already seen how meat was as much a hipster cultural icon as beards and tattoos. The foie gras burger and poutine with oxtail gravy at Animal on Fairfax Avenue were harbingers.

In New York that summer, upmarket left-wing food retailer Whole Foods Market took over a park for Meatopia, described as 'Meatopia 2012: the City of Meat' or 'Woodstock of Edible Animals'. It was set on Randalls Island, a park between Harlem and Queens on the East River, where the massive space was divided into districts, with names like Meatopia Heights, Game Reserve, Carcass Hill, Beaktown and Offalwood. With big-name sponsors like global alcohol manufacturer Diageo on board, the original ethical-meat message was somehow lost and Meatopia was a hedonistic festival of flesh. Even the personified steer on the poster had a knowing look that suggested it not only knew it was going to be eaten but wanted to be.

Politically speaking, the overt eating of meat had been a twentieth-century affirmation of the right to freedom. Even a right-wing affair. At Meatopia 2012 the confluence of ethical meat and celebratory feasting on it converged, mingling the right wing with the left. The red with the blue. So at the end of the day, the right to eat as much meat as you want, as long as it is raised ethically, paints those who cling to those beliefs a strange shade of purple.

In the hipster gift shop I picked up a jigsaw puzzle box. On it was a landscape made from meat. There were hills in the distance made from ham, a pancetta waterfall cascading into a bacon lake. By its shores sat a wiener log cabin shaded by mortadella trees and corn dog shrubs. It was a grotesque meat-based pastiche with a nod to the fantasy works of Pieter Bruegel the Elder, a Flemish Renaissance painter who created *The Land of Cockaigne*, a Reformation predecessor of 'Big Rock Candy Mountain'. Both are fantasy lands of plentiful food everywhere, where there is no need for work, as the very fabric of the earth is edible. In Bruegel's work a peasant, a soldier and a cleric are asleep under a tree, the fences to the fields are made of interwoven sausages, a pig runs about with a knife in its back ready to slice away the flesh, a cottage is thatched with pies, and loaves of bread form themselves into a shrubbery. Bruegel painted in a time of frequent famine and major social, religious and political upheaval. The smallgoods-landscape jigsaw puzzle, executed in photoshop, was presumably an ironic reminder of excess and surplus. It had been reduced from $35 to $8.

Outside I wandered past the Soulfood Café. There was a noticeable difference. It was quieter, not as cluttered. I wandered in and looked at the menu. It was breakfast time and there was ham and eggs on the menu. Ethically sourced meat had made its way into one of the great bastions of vegetarianism. 'Times have changed,' said the waitress. 'Smith Street has changed so much. So we had to move with the times.' After more than a decade, this meat-free café had sold its soul.

FAUX PAS

A vegetarian acquaintance who was aware of my previous predilection for flesh suggested I try a Chinese restaurant that specialised in mock meat.

Squashed into what had once been an office furniture showroom near the casino, the restaurant was lit by clammy green fluorescent light. Only the chopsticks on the table and Chinese vases on dark wooden furniture gave a touch of Oriental hospitality. Michael Bublé crooned through the house PA. The big band backing and live crowd sounded small and tinny. On a plate in front of me was a bowl of shark's fin soup. Faux shark's fin soup. Just like the sesame prawn toast served next, it was a fake. As was the barbecued pork and braised ginger duck. Every dish in this Chinese vegetarian restaurant was fake.

Not a forgery or an interpretation, but fakes. The maker had studied the originals and then done everything in their power to reproduce them. Except the bit about meat. It was like a perfectly reproduced version of Monet's waterlilies, with every brushstroke placed in exactly the same place on the canvas. Except once it was in the mouth, you realised the forger was using acrylic paint instead of oils.

According to the restaurant's mantra published on its website, it serves strictly vegetarian food based on mock meat. It explains that the restaurant's mock-meat products are 'intended to broaden the vegetarian dining experience and encourage those who would like to make the transition to a meatless lifestyle, without necessarily giving up the taste and texture' of meat. Mock meat is actually a range of soy proteins and wheat gluten that has been flavoured, coloured and textured to resemble different flesh. The visible likeness is uncanny. With suspension of disbelief, you could almost be forgiven for mistaking it for the real thing. Almost. Just like the waxworks in Madame Tussauds almost look like the flesh-and-blood creatures they are modelled on.

The concept of mock meat is not new. It is ancient. Early Chinese emperors were required to eschew meat for seven weeks every year prior to taking part in prayers to ensure the prosperity of the kingdom. Over time his chefs created a repertoire of dishes that resembled the meaty original but were made with other substances that resembled flesh, both visually, texturally and flavour-wise. The techniques have survived and are kept alive by Buddhist monks, some of whom still cook from scratch. There are huge businesses in Asia based on the production of mock meat.

A journey around health-food shops and grocers put me face to face with what to me were novel foods. Naturally I had to taste them and find out how they were made. Some of the faux flesh is made with tofu. This is a food-manufacturing technique that is over 2000 years old. Soybeans are cooked in water to make a milk. A coagulant is added and the protein clumps together to form curd. The curd is pressed to remove liquid and you're left with tofu that can be flavoured and formed into different shapes.

Then there is TVP. Sounds like an Eastern European fast train, but it is actually textured vegetable protein. This is a beige substance made from the material left over from soybeans once they have been processed for oil extraction. The fibre and protein is turned into a slurry and heated to 200 degrees Celsius to denature the proteins. It's extruded through a nozzle and when it hits the air the change in pressure makes it expand to become a light, spongy material. It can be formed into different shapes, and flavoured with stuff that makes it yummy—generally, vegetable extracts and amino acids. Because of its low cost of production and long shelf life in its dehydrated form, it is used in the fast-food industry to bulk out processed meats.

One of the products made from soy that I was enticed to buy was mock bacon. Still wary that real bacon could be my downfall, I searched out an ersatz vegan bacon not so much to eat but so as simply to know it existed in case I had a bout of post-carnivore bacon cravings. I found a product we will call VegO Bacon Ham. It came in a simple plastic vacuum-sealed bag—two pre-sliced blocks of square matter that looked like pink luncheon ham complete with fat-like flecks of white. It was heavy and moist like processed pork, and the bag, when sliced open, revealed a slightly smoky aroma incompletely concealing a smell vaguely similar to that of a tyre showroom. Moist and meaty in the mouth, the texture was almost exactly the same as defrosted frozen bacon. The aroma coming up the back of the mouth into the nostrils was vaguely meaty, but it was more like opening the box of a spare tube when fixing a puncture on a bike. The tongue and mouth were saying meat but the olfactory system was screaming, 'OIL SPILL! OIL SPILL! PETROCHEMICAL ALERT!' It was as if the VegO Bacon Ham had been 3D-printed by a computer—the programmers had spent all their time getting the texture and look right, and when it came to flavour, they simply inserted the code for thongs.

The concept that soy-based meat-free meat substitutes are a step towards upward moral mobility is entrenched in the advertising and marketing of these products. The next bacon I tried was branded VegeFarm but when I looked up the company's location on a satellite map, I saw the VegeFarm is in a modern industrial estate in Gueishan, Taiwan. The ingredients list read that the bacon was made from soy protein, a protein often isolated from the residue of soy meal after the extraction of oil. Next is whey protein, a byproduct of cheesemaking or from milk processing. It also contains canola oil, starch and glucomannan, a sticky starch-like polysaccharide derived from the roots of a tropical plant. The next ingredient is curdlan. This is a polymer of glucose, or lots of glucose molecules joined together that when heated form a water-retaining gel. Curdlan is made from a bacteria, often found in the human body, responsible for urinary tract infections. My bacon ham also contained salt, sugar, a substance called 'vegetable seasoning' and another called 'vegetarian essence'. 'Vegetarian essence', I can reassure you, is made from hydrolysed vegetable protein and not actual vegetarians. The lovely pink tinge of my bacon ham comes from FD & C Red#40. This is a red food dye derived from petro chemicals, banned in several countries and not recommend for children in the European Union. But not one animal died in its making.

Millions of living cells died, however, to make my Quorn fajita strips. Moist, spongy and coated in a sweet, faintly perfumed coating, these meat-free pieces of food were made from mycoprotein derived from a fungus called *Fusarium venenatum*. If you concentrate, it does taste vaguely mushroomy, like the blandest of camembert. Quorn was born in the 1960s at the same time the green revolution was kicking in. The green revolution is the name given to the transfer of industrial, technical, chemical and organisational practices from industry to agriculture after World War I. This saw the reorganisation of land use across Europe, North America, Australasia and parts of Asia from small-scale food production to more broad-scale, mechanised production that exponentially increased food production. Quorn was envisaged by British industrialist J Arthur Rank, the same man who formed the Rank film production company. He instructed his team at milling and baking company Rank Hovis McDougall to investigate making high-protein food for humans from fungus. At that time there was a serious burgeoning global food supply problem, with demand outweighing supply, and the threat of widespread food shortages. Rank Hovis McDougall, together with Imperial Chemical

Industries (ICI), isolated *Fusarium venenatum* from the soil where it grows as a white spiderweb-like filament. It was grown in fermenting tanks on a solution of glucose derived from corn and essential minerals, with the fungus filtered out in a continuous process. Early production success was met with regulatory suspicion. Some types of *Fusarium* produced mycotoxins (mushroom poisons) so it took until the mid-1980s for the mycoprotein derived from this safe version of *Fusarium* to be approved for human consumption. Blended with egg white and other compounds for flavour and texture, the product was ready for the market. Except the market was not ready for it. It took until the mid-1990s, and the personal intervention of businessman Lord Sainsbury, for it to be listed on British supermarket shelves. It rolled out across the globe, only arriving in Australia in 2010. Quorn's moist sponginess and flavour, added as an afterthought, make it appealing to those who are truly hungry.

More convincing, however, are the mock meats made from wheat gluten. You'll understand what wheat gluten is if you have ever tried to clean cooking utensils after making bread. If you soak a mixing bowl with a little leftover bread dough in it, the water will wash away the starch while leaving the more tenacious gluten. Gluten is formed by wheat proteins that come together to form big, long strands as you knead the dough. Try to scrub gluten strands off and they do their best to form more elastic and rubbery shapes and forms. When thin sheets of the gluten are laid one on top of each other, they not only stick together but also do a reasonable job of looking like layers of muscle found in duck breasts. When the gluten has Chinese five-spice, ginger and 'vegetarian seasoning' added to it, the flavours begin to align with braised duck. Marinate the stuff in soy sauce and its dark amino acids take it from pallid beige to pleasing deep brown. Give it some time on hot metal with a little oil and, in a certain light, it could be braised duck. The same process is used to make mock chicken, abalone, beef and lamb.

The process of refining protein from wheat is not unique to Asia. In the south of Lebanon during the annual *mouneh*, or harvest month, in autumn, women, mainly, go about harvesting and curing food to last over winter. This is a time when sausages are fermented and smoked, olives are picked and brined and wheat cheese is made. This is made from wheat dough that is washed of its starch, with the gluten rolled into balls and dried like Lebanese shanklish cheese. These balls are then stored, with herbs, in olive oil. I learned about this from the man who ran the farmers' market in Beirut, Lebanon. Kamal Mouzawak explained to me by phone how the women in the south of the country made 'vegan cheese' every autumn, but in some areas close to the border with Israel, the thousands-of-years-old tradition had stopped in recent years, due to the last Israeli incursion. Although I have never eaten 'vegan cheese' from Lebanon, I have eaten some other wheat-based vegetarian foods.

One was a gourmet meat-free mince with a delicious-looking image on the cardboard cover of the box of a nest of creamy white spaghetti mounted with a chunky tomato and onion rich sauce. I slid out the clear plastic box inside to reveal a mass of what looked like engorged Weeties. Brown amorphous flakes of 'delicious, mouthwatering alternative to meat'. This stuff was made from both soy and wheat gluten, vegetable oil, soy protein, textured wheat protein, ground flax, natural flavouring, salt, malt extract, dried yeast, unrefined sugar, carrageenan, zinc sulphate and vitamin B6. Similar to what I imagine Soylent Green looks like, it is made in the same Midlands industrial estate in the United Kingdom as Avon cosmetics and Aquascutum coats.

The brown not-meat had a friend on the shelf that, judging by the packet, was going to give me a fish experience similar to any UK Friday-night dinner in front of the telly. Without the fish. Meat-free fish fingers, chips and peas. These 'meat-free fish style fingers' captured the experience of factory-processed crumbed fish extremely well, replicating the golden crumb and moist interior that, although made of soy protein, still managed to taste like the way a fish-processing facility smells. It's amazing what they can do with food these days.

Despite Quorn, TVP and food made from soy and other vegetable products marketing themselves as happy meat-free, soy-free alternatives, they are, at their very heart, still factory food. And because the process hides the origin, they evoke my suspicion. Quorn, for example, takes a traditional non-food species into factories and breeds them up to form a medium to which flavours and textures are added to make it palatable. It is then pressed into forms that resemble foods we know. Quorn and other non-meat proteins like tofu, textured vegetable protein and wheat gluten mock meats are formed into meat-like shapes to resemble sausages, bacon, ham, salami. Because they undergo this unnatural transformation, many people trust them as they would trust any shapeshifter. Shapeshifters are archetypes from mythology. From Gilgamesh to werewolves to terrifying sci-fi creatures such as the bad cop in *Terminator*, they instil in us a fear and suspicion of things that have been transformed from one thing to resemble another. And despite how much the manufacturers try to make mock meats look like the fleshy, platonic ideal, they are destined to fail because of the high expectation they set up for the food to taste like the real thing. Vegan sausages. Tofurky. Quorn chicken-style nuggets. These are simply meat-free analogues of flesh fast food. They are fodder for the food illiterate, people who have never learned to cook, people who were taught that food will fall from the factory conveyor belt into their mouths as long as their mouths and wallets are open.

Mock meats truly frighten me. They are marketed with names expressing freedom and enlightenment, yet in reality are hallmarks that the diner has given up all sovereignty to understanding cooking and food, and enslaved themselves further and deeper to the industrial complex.

Back in the Chinese restaurant, my dish of mock Malaysian lamb curry had arrived. The blocks of mock lamb were commendably artful in their mimicry of real chunks of lamb shoulder, right down to individual stray fibres of vegetable protein sticking out of the stuff. This was sitting in a lovely grey-brown slurry with a pool of red oil floating on top. It reminded me of every Malaysian lamb curry I had ever eaten. It was curry, but not as we know it. The star protein was an impostor. As I dipped the roti bread into the sauce, Michael Bublé continued his polished croon.

7

Meat Eaters from Outer Space

Out in Central Victoria, nestled along the Goulburn River, is the historic town of Murchison. It is quite a beautiful little town that has had a long association with incarceration. Nearby was an Aboriginal protectorate, another name for a concentration camp, for the Goulburn Valley Aboriginal people. One of them, King Charles Tattambo, is buried in the local cemetery, on a small ridge slightly elevated above the local settlers. His brass nameplate has been soldered to his grave. Across the cemetery is an ossuary, a stone building that looks as if it would be more at home in the mountains above Milan than Murchison. This is the final resting place for the bones of Italian prisoners of the prisoner-of-war camps that dotted the countryside during World War II.

Just off Murchison's main drag is the Murchison and District Historical Society Museum, housed in a nondescript brown brick building that somehow reminds me of Chocolate Ripple Biscuits. Inside sits a piece of coal-black rock safely secured in a thick glass case. On loan from the Chicago Field Museum, it is a 400-gram shard that broke off from a meteorite that exploded above the town and surrounding farmland one

Sunday morning in 1969. 'We were getting ready for church,' remembered Robyn Trickey. Her memories are recorded in documents in the museum. 'We went outside to see what we thought was a jet aeroplane. The dogs were barking in the kennel. The cows came running home.' There was a roar outside that some said sounded like a bushfire, or a jet engine breaking through the sound barrier. Those outside looked up to see a smoke trail following a bright light in the sky. The meteorite broke up in the lower atmosphere, showering the district with lumps of black rock. Despite nearly 100 kilograms of rock hitting the earth at supersonic speed, the only casualties were a tree branch, a piece of corrugated iron and a handrail in a milking shed.

The Trickey family kept their piece under a glass dome. Every time they lifted the dome they were struck by a strong smell, like that of methylated spirits. There was something inside the Murchison meteorite, the black rock covered in a hardened molten skin, that was drawing scientists from Melbourne, then Sydney, then all over the world. Quietly they would arrive at weekends, when people were at home, and ask if they had any of the meteorite or if they could scour their land to find some. 'The locals didn't understand the significance of what had landed on the town,' Kay Ball, president of the Murchison and District Historical Society, told me. 'So everyone innocently handed the shards of rock, some weighing well over several kilograms, over to the visitors.' Within months almost every shard of the rock had been quietly whisked away to laboratories across the globe. The scientists were breaking down the meteorite to find out exactly what was inside it. What they discovered rocked the scientific world and provided evidence for a new theory: Life On Earth Originated In Outer Space.

Professor John Lovering described the experience in an interview with Melbourne Museum in 2012 for their Dynamic Earth exhibition. He was a professor of geology at Melbourne University at the time. 'We got some of the samples and immediately we analysed [them]. Later on people started to do work on the organic composition of the meteorite, in which there's about … 2% organic material … and about 10% water. A lot of funny things that you don't find normally in meteorites. And the exciting thing is there has been the complexity of the organic compounds they found; many amino acids … the building blocks of life itself—are all present in this meteorite.' Over the years more than seventy amino acids have been identified from within the meteorite. Of these, only nineteen are known from earth. The complexity of these and other organic compounds present in the meteorite demonstrate that the simple chemical building blocks necessary for life on earth can form in other places. This discovery was grist to the mill of scientists working on theories that life on earth was 'seeded' by meteorites such as the one that landed at Murchison.

What Professor Lovering found amazing was that all the building blocks for life, including amino acids, were to be found on a rock that came from outer space. One of the amino acids Lovering was referring to was glutamic acid. It is a string of carbon, hydrogen, nitrogen and oxygen atoms that form a compound that is an essential neurotransmitter in the brain. Without it we wouldn't have memory. Without memory, what are we? Glutamic acid is also detected by your tongue. We detect it as a savoury, brothy, mouth-filling, pleasant sensation. It is one of the compounds that the tongue detects, giving us the sensation of savoury or, as the Japanese like to call it, 'umami'. It sits alongside the sensations of saltiness, sweetness, acid and bitterness. Glutamic acid exists in the planet's yummiest foods: parmesan cheese, dashi, mushroom, and meat—chicken, seafood, lamb, beef and pork. Glutamic acid is, in a word, delicious.

That a compound from outer space could be delicious struck me as remarkable. Why can our tongues detect glutamic acid but not, say, glass? Why can we taste monosaccharides and disaccharides—sugars—and not polysaccharides, which we know as starch? They are all carbohydrates.

A visit to one of the nation's leading experts on the tongue and how it works unlocked the world of taste for me, with a few simple experiments. Russell Keast PhD is a professor at the Department of Exercise and Nutrition Science at the Centre for Physical Activity and Nutrition Research at Melbourne's Deakin University. He's an affable Kiwi who likes craft beer and good food. He put me through one of his regular taste tests that he applies to hundreds of people in order to gain raw data on how the human tongue detects compounds that we understand as 'taste'.

Standing in his taste lab—all stainless steel benches, fridges of food, and lines and lines of tiny cups filled with small amounts of colourless liquids—Keast told me, 'You know that tongue map you were taught at school. Well, it's wrong. Mostly. There was a misinterpretation of a diagram developed in Germany in the early twentieth century. We have different tastebuds that can detect different compounds that we perceive as salty, sweet, sour, bitter and umami.' He explained that although some of our tastebuds are more concentrated in some areas than others, we generally perceive all five tastes on all areas of the tongue. He was quick to point out, however, an essential point that anyone working in the food and wine industry needs to understand. 'Not everyone tastes everything in the same way. Thirty per cent of people don't detect bitterness very well,' he said. 'About the same percentage of people don't detect umami unless they are trained to do so. Some people are very sensitive to saltiness and bitterness,' he went on. 'And, although it is not strictly a taste issue, 13 per cent of people not only don't like coriander—to them, it is disgusting. It tastes like soap.' When a herb that so many people love the flavour of is repugnant to a small but not insignificant proportion of the population, this poses real conundrums for chefs and diners alike.

His assistant ushered me into a dimly lit room full of booths partitioned off from each other. In front of me was a pen and paper. A hole appeared in the wall and a tray covered in rows of eight little plastic cups in a line was pushed towards me. Each cup contained an anonymous compound dissolved in water that would stimulate certain tastebuds. From left to right, each cup contained a little more of the compound than the previous one. I had to make a mark on the sheet of paper when I detected something on my tongue, and then make another mark when I knew what each cup contained. Sugar was easy. I caught on to that one in the eight cups pretty early on. Next up was acid—citric acid, I reckoned. I could detect that in small amounts. Bitterness—I am king. I could taste the bitter compound, what I learned later was a tiny drop of liquid caffeine diluted in a lot of water. When it came to salt it took me quite a few tastes in the line of cups before I could not only detect a difference but also work out exactly what it was that I was tasting. Not a good sign for my cardiovascular future. Then came the last set of cups to taste. It took four cups for me to realise that the water tasted, well, delicious. Clear, colourless water. But incredibly delicious.

Back in Keast's lab it was revealed to me that the water was delicious because it was seasoned with dissolved monosodium glutamate, also known as E621 or MSG. This is a synthesised version of the naturally occurring compound glutamic acid, first isolated from wheat gluten in the late nineteenth century by German scientist Karl Ritthausen. Glutamic acid was again isolated from kelp, in the early 1900s, by Kikunae Ikeda, a researcher at the Tokyo Imperial University. He made kombu broth and concentrated it. Kombu is a type of kelp and a cornerstone ingredient, along with dried tuna, of the Japanese stock dashi. The tuna is not only dried but often fermented. Despite being a fine broth it is deceptively rich and very tasty. In it are several amino acids, which we find delicious. Glutamic acid is found in vegetables such as capsicum, potato and tomato. Many fungi, such as field mushrooms, porcini and oyster mushrooms, are good sources of it. Many fermented products, such as kimchi and salami, are high in glutamates, not only from the smaller amounts in the body of the substance being fermented but also from the little yeast cells that are doing the fermentation. Other compounds high in glutamates are fermented animal proteins such as cheese, jamón and anchovies, in which various fungi, bacteria or enzymes break down proteins into amino acids such as glutamic acid. Flesh in general is high in glutamic acid—not as high as preserved flesh, such as prosciutto, salami and cured fish, but still high enough to register as 'delicious' when it hits one's tastebuds.

Another amino acid is aspartic acid, found in vegetables such as asparagus, which causes a similar savoury sensation in most people. This was one of the amino acids found in the Murchison meteorite.

That we are hardwired to detect and enjoy compounds formed in outer space but found in nutritious food has evolutionary advantages. As do all the compounds detected on the tongue. The neural pathways for our sense of taste were laid down in utero. Basically, nerves join our tastebuds to travel to the brain stem—the lizard part of our brain. We are hardwired to taste and don't even need to think about it. It just happens.

We are hardwired to taste salt because without it we die. (Eat too much salt and you die too, but that's another story). Salt is essential for the chemical reactions in our bodies. Think about proto-humans, primates who sourced all their food directly from nature without the intervention of any annoying modern conveniences, such as agriculture, mechanised food production or transportation. Unless you're living by the shore, next to a salt lake or close to a seam of exposed subterranean salt, you're going to need to find salt from the world around you. Salt occurs in small quantities in nature, in some plants, and is something we can source from the flesh and blood of other animals. Having the ability to detect a compound essential to survival by simply putting your tongue on it is a pretty cool tool to have.

An organ that can detect energy in an energy-scarce world is also a handy tool to have. Our tongues are equipped with tastebuds that can detect about a tenth of a teaspoon of sugar (disaccharide) dissolved in a cup of water. More simple sugars, such as fruit sugar (fructose, a monosaccharide) and honey (a mix of two monosaccharides—glucose and fructose), we can detect at marginally higher concentrations. These are all compounds that are packed with molecules the human body can easily untangle and burn as fuel, or turn into fat for later use. In other words, our tongues detect compounds with energy and we love the taste.

But wait! There's more! Our tongues are like Swiss Army knives helping us survive the poisonous arsenal produced by plants in self-defence. Our sense of bitterness is hardwired for survival and is our first line of protection against poison. Many poisonous plants have evolved to produce alkaloids to guard themselves from pest attack. We detect alkaloids as bitter. Unlike mild saltiness, bitterness is generally unpleasant. Many brightly coloured berries are poisonous, but many others are nutritious. A human who can detect bitterness in small quantities is a good human to have around in a small group of hunter-gatherers. On the flip side, some of our favourite pastimes involve consuming bitter substances. Beer is bitter. Coffee is bitter, as is tea, thanks to the caffeine and tannin. Wine can have bitterness. Chewing tobacco is bitter, as is chewing hashish. It seems the bitter substances we have become most fond of have rewarded other parts of our brains with chemical versions of excitement or pleasure.

Theories on why we have evolved with an acid-detecting tongue are a little more complex. Award-winning wine writer Max Allen hypothesises that the human tongue evolved to detect changes in pH in liquids. This was an indicator that very ripe fruit had gone beyond its optimum ripeness and begun to ferment. Alcohol is an energy-dense food and therefore desirable to proto-humans in an energy-scarce world. Although I strongly support Allen's theory, there are those who suggest that acid detection alerts us that food is of such a low pH that it could disrupt the efficient digestion of food if eaten. Or, in the words of my mother when she somehow knew we were going off to filch apples, 'Don't eat the unripe ones, as they'll give you a tummy ache'.

As far as a palate hardwired for compounds that are 'delicious', the theory seems to be that although the human body can synthesise non-essential amino acids such as glutamate, these are often found in conjunction with other amino acids that are not as tasty but are essential to our wellbeing. For example, crab is delicious. The compound that gives crab its unique taste is an amino acid called arginine. Arginine in itself is quite bitter, but in crab it is also found with glutamate. Together they are delicious. Sea urchin is a similarly delicious living creature, which contains another bitter amino acid called methionine. But sea urchin is also packed with glutamic acid. The body cannot synthesise methionine as it can glutamic acid. The fact glutamic acid occurs so frequently alongside other amino acids seems to be the common factor. While we don't necessarily need to eat glutamate, as the body makes its own, it is found alongside essential amino acids that we do need and can't make ourselves.

At this point it is probably important to point out that MSG is a salt of glutamic acid and is made from plant extracts to form translucent crystals that are used extensively in the food industry as a flavour enhancer.

The amazing thing about our ability to detect deliciousness is that it is easily manipulated to create an overwhelming sense of umami. There are two other truly delicious amino acids commonly found in the food we eat. Other tasty, non-essential amino acids are guanylate and inosinate. When they are combined together or with glutamate, they can overwhelm the tongue, lips and cheeks with an enduring and lingering sense of pleasure that some find analogous to coital overload.

This is a synergistic effect that is common knowledge for and second nature to Japanese chefs but is just dawning upon almost all Western chefs. In the north-east Victorian town of Beechworth, chef and former chemist Michael Ryan explained to me a little of the science behind why these amino acids make food taste good. 'Seaweed, particularly kelp, is naturally high in an amino acid called glutamate,' he said in quiet, measured words. 'Combine kombu with dried shiitake mushrooms, which are high in guanylate—another amino acid—or with bonito, which is high in inosinate, and something amazing happens,' he said. 'There is a synergy between these natural compounds that gives you a very strong sensation of umami. The effect is remarkable.' Ryan proves this in his dish of kingfish poached in dashi and then brushed with *iwa-nori*, a jam made by cooking down nori sheets with sake and sugar. This is served with a salad of cucumber and sea spaghetti, seaweed that is imported from Spain, plus a little of a native seaweed grown on a farm in East Gippsland. It is sensational. Similar effects are achieved when cheese is washed down with cider, the yeast cells releasing glutamate upon their demise. Classic matches include asparagus served with parmesan cheese. Avocado and tomato. Anchovies and sherry. Four 'N Twenty pie and sauce.

This line of investigation had proved so fruitful; some areas of exploration are dead-end rabbit holes. This little journey into the role of amino acids in our diet had uncovered the most profound idea. Life on earth possibly started with organic compounds that landed on it on rocks from outer space; we are all born with organs that can taste those rocks and we find those rocks delicious.

Before I left Professor Keast he sent me on one last quest. Back in the booth I had eight little cups in front of me. I tasted each one, rolling the cool liquid over my tongue. After the fourth I paused. It was different, but I didn't recognise the taste. A slightly tingling sensation on the tongue, but not one of the other five taste sensations. With each cup the sensation grew stronger. I could 'taste' something but couldn't tell what it was. 'That's fat,' explained Professor Keast. 'We haven't proved it yet but I think it won't be long and we will have enough data to put forward in an academic paper that the human tongue can detect fat. Imagine the implications of that.'

It was in February 2015 that Keast and his team made the announcement to the world. Fat was the sixth taste. He published a paper in the peer-reviewed journal *Flavour*.

After half a decade's research and subjecting 500 volunteers to taste trials, Professor Keast proved the human tongue had tastebuds that could detect the presence of fatty acids at levels as low as ten parts per million. He said at the time, 'We were using oleic acid that is found in many everyday foods such as olive oil, canola oil, meat and dairy products.' Subjects were placed in isolated booths, the same as the one he had placed me in earlier, and asked to taste clear cups of water into which was placed tiny amounts of fatty acid. Around 40 per cent of people detected the fatty acid at very low levels, around ten parts per million, and this figure increased to 80 per cent at 100 parts per million. Keast said the detection of fat by tongue does not give a 'conscious perception of taste quality such as sweet or saltiness'; instead, participants in experiments could detect a different sensation on their tongue.

'In high concentrations of fatty acids, subjects reported an unpleasant sensation,' Keast said. 'We [scientists] think that this could be an evolutionary response signalling that the fat in the food may have broken down over time and not be fresh or nutritious.' It is interesting to note that many people cannot consciously detect the sensation of umami or savouriness unless they are trained to do so. Perhaps, with training, we will be able to be conscious of the sensation of fat on our tongues on a day-to-day basis. Keast suggested that people who detect fatty acids also associate the taste sensation with the feeling of being full and that people who have difficulty in detecting fatty acids are often obese. Sensitivity to fatty acids can be increased by going on a low-fat diet, after which the ability to detect fatty acids increases and, by association, the ability to feel full.

An extra taste is an amazing discovery. It is as if science detected another colour that sat between yellow and green on the spectrum. A colour that had been there all along that we simply hadn't been trained to see. I have practised to see if I can taste fat. It's hard. You have to really concentrate, as there is so much other information going on in the mouth and nose. It's as if we're not really meant to be able to recognise it. The sensation pops up when I least expect it. Eating a store-bought biscuit. Chewing oats in muesli. The lingering tingling after eating something with egg mayo. The sensation is not always there but, like many things in life, once you learn about it, you can never unlearn it.

8

Umami by Numbers

After my brush with the extraterrestrial and fat tastebuds, it was time to come back down to earth and put some newly learned theory into practice. Knowing that we naturally crave umami, I set out to look at ways of identifying sources of umami in the meat-free world.

One of the most common sources of umami in the average kitchen is the humble tomato. It contains 120 milligrams of the savoury-tasting amino acid glutamate per 100 grams. A fully ripe tomato, harvested ripe on the vine, can contain as much as 270 milligrams of glutamate per 100 grams. A tomato harvested pink then gas-ripened will contain around 70 milligrams per 100 grams. This little measurement of glutamate helps explain why supermarket tomatoes, and other veg, are not as delicious as they used to be. Supermarket tomatoes are not harvested when vine ripe but when ripe enough to reach the 'correct' colour by the time they are trucked, stored and sent to the supermarket. The level of glutamate rises as the tomato ripens. When a ripe tomato is dried, the flavour is concentrated even further and you can end up with a whopping 620 milligrams of glutamate per 100 grams. This is getting close to Cabrales cheese, a blue cheese from Spain, at 760 milligrams per 100 grams. One of the most intense umami hits you can have in your fridge is parmesan cheese, which weighs in at a mighty 1200 milligrams per 100 grams.

Other everyday vegetables contain these 'delicious' compounds, but to a lesser extent. Potatoes and cabbage contain 100 milligrams per 100 grams, and carrots 30 milligrams per 100 grams. When vegetables are cooked, however, this ratio can double. This is because when vegetables are sautéed, fried, stewed and baked they lose moisture—or water. This is what chef Jacques Reymond was referring to earlier in this book. 'Cooking down' or 'reducing' a dish, in kitchen language, means heating it so the water evaporates. When vegetables are reduced by cooking, the ratio of glutamic acid therefore increases. When vegetables are reduced they become more delicious. This was explained to me by a Catalan chef a few years prior to my beginning *My Year Without Meat*.

I was in the relatively remote village of Falset near the famous wine-growing region of Priorat, south of Barcelona, where chef Roger Felip had a restaurant called Mas Trucafort. It is perched in a relatively high valley in the Montsant mountains, looking out on the Ebro River below. When I visited, it was a cool day with a chance of rain and we were making paella under the cover of his shed. The walls were made with the same slatey stone that forms the famous *llicorella*, the stony soil in which the bush vines of this region manage to produce such outstanding wine. Roger had stacked logs from old olive trees around the walls. He is well known for his indoor/outdoor, all-weather paellas. Rice dishes are found throughout Spain. The most famous seafood paella, laden with prawns and mussels, is the paella valenciana. In other regions, paellas are made with whatever is in season and available. Roger had lit a small fire in a rustic open fireplace built into the back wall. The fire was now building in size and strength as Roger fed it with handfuls of dried grape vines. He placed a *paellera* on top. This is the flat pan in which the paella is made, and after which it is named. On top of this he started his *sofregit*, which is Catalan for *sofrito*. This is the jam-like tomato and red pepper base used to add the rich intensity to paella. Into the *paellera* went a vast amount of extra virgin olive oil from his own grove. Into this an entire head of garlic was placed. He added a handful of wild thyme pulled from the rocks where it was growing at the back of the shed. He pushed these around in the oil. The intention was to flavour the oil. These ingredients were removed after fifteen minutes or so, when the garlic was well and truly brown and the thyme had disintegrated. He then threw in handfuls of uniformly chopped pieces of red and yellow peppers that sizzled in the hot, aromatic oil. They were slowly cooked down until they were soft and deeper red and gold. To this were added chopped ripe tomatoes, which hit the hot metal and let out a last defiant hiss as they gave up their juice. All these actions were dispensed with a deft, almost subliminal, addition of salt.

The fire died down and the vegetables simmered away, reducing to a dark, sticky, jam-like *sofregit*. 'Try it,' insisted Roger, offering a dessertspoon from his back pocket. It was good. It was really good. It was greater than the sum of its parts. Sweet with a lovely sharp finish, it had an overwhelming sense of savouriness that was memorable, as are so many of the dishes from the Iberian Peninsula that start with a slow reduction of vegetables.

While the Spanish, and Catalans for that matter, understand instinctively how to incorporate that savouriness in their cooking, they don't have a specific term for it. To them it is simply *delicioso*. Delicious.

They are not the only culture to have developed a cooked and reduced base. You will find this layering and cooking down of vegetables in so many cuisines. Many French dishes start with mirepoix. This is a medium dice of celery, carrot and onion that is often sautéed in butter or oil (or rendered animal fat) to create the base of the dish. Depending on the region, the vegetables are given some colour with a fast sauté, or allowed to cook under their own steam over lower heat and with a lid on. As other ingredients are added, the vegetables release their 'flavour' into the cooking liquid, which is reduced as the dish cooks. It is this process of addition and reduction that increases the flavour. It's a numbers game.

Similar bases are found in Italian cooking. The Italian *sofrito* is basically mirepoix with the addition of garlic. (Italian food nationalists—yes, they exist—always like to remind the world that France did not have a cuisine until Catherine de' Medici married Prince Henry of France and took her entourage, including cooks, with her, thus introducing 'proper' food to France.) The French royal family was not the only royal household to be infiltrated by the Italians. Polish king Sigismund I the Old married Bona Sforza, an Italian. This is why many Polish dishes start with włoszczyzna. This means 'greens' and refers to the base of many soups and stews made with carrots, parsnips, celery, leek, and sometimes, cabbage. Similarly, the Germans start soups and stews with *Suppengrün*. This means 'soup greens' and refers to a mix of leek, carrot, and sometimes, celeriac—a variety of celery appreciated for its engorged root and not the stems. It can also include one, some or all of the following: swede, onion, parsley leaves, parsley roots, thyme and celery leaves. The ingredients can be removed before serving, allowed to cook down to the point of creating a thick sauce, or served whole as part of the finished dish.

The idea is to create an intense vegetable stock. As the vegetables give up their liquid they also give up their water-soluble nutrients and flavour compounds, including acids and sugars. Note that starchy vegetables, such as potato, are not included in these flavour bases, as the starch would thicken the dish prematurely.

So with this new understanding of the process of layering and reducing vegetables during cooking, I approached the preparation of meals with a newfound zeal. I re-embraced a huge swathe of traditional dishes made without meat that combine different vegetables to create deliciousness. The summer vegetable braise from the south of France, ratatouille, sees onions, tomato, pepper, eggplant and zucchini gently cooked together. The addition of an egg cooked in the sauce makes a meal. Bubble-and-squeak is a classic English dish and an amazingly transmogrifying one, that turns the most unappealing leftover vegetables into a delicious rustic vegetable pancake with a crisp and caramelised crust folded through it. Colcannon is ostensibly a poverty dish from Ireland, of potatoes, cabbage, shallots, cream and butter. When brought together, these ingredients create a warming and tasty embrace.

Another evergreen in the flavour arsenal are sauces made from fermented foods—the breakdown of proteins releasing amino acids and sometimes yeast, adding a little umami, too. It is this breakdown of proteins through cooking or fermentation that creates these incredibly tasty combinations. I was standing in Nan Yang, a Chinese–Vietnamese supermarket owned by an elderly matriarch, Chi Yao, who arrived in Australia as a boat person in 1979. There was an entire double-sided, tightly stacked aisle filled with diverse sauces and condiments derived from protein and packed with delicious glutamates. Soy sauce, mushroom sauce, tonkatsu sauce, teriyaki sauce, oyster sauce (not vegetarian), tamari, hoisin, fish sauce (made from fermented fish guts and not vegetarian), Kewpie mayonnaise (made with processed oil and lots of MSG), sriracha chilli sauce (made with red chillies, themselves a good source of glutamate). It was literally a wall of umami made mostly by fermentation.

I really love salads. Not lettuce and cucumber dressed with vinaigrette, but great big plates of vegetables that are meals in themselves. The secret is to layer umami-rich vegetables—such as asparagus, avocado and mushrooms—in raw salads and make a dressing with an umami-rich sauce, such as soy sauce balanced with lemon or lime juice, and perhaps a splash of sesame oil. With the combination of veg and dressing, you get that umami hit. Yummy and quite decadent dishes include cauliflower cheese (the addition of a vego stock cube to the sauce is a revelation, although a culinary transgression for purists) and potatoes cooked in a sauce made with onions, garlic and tomatoes. If you're still hungry for umami after that, have a cup of good-quality Japanese green tea—with a whopping 668 milligrams of glutamate per 100 grams. Enjoy.

Dried kelp—the Japanese call it kombu, and use it in making dashi—can hit levels of over 3000 milligrams of glutamate per 100 grams. While not reaching these stellar concentrations of glutamate, its more common cousin is nori. You will know this as sushi sheets. It's a type of sea algae that is cleaned, dried, reformed into fine sheets and packaged. It is really good for making vegetarian chicken salt—chicken salt being salt, hydrolysed protein or MSG and seasonings. Take a pack of nori sheets and break them with your hands, then place in a high-speed blender. A Thermomix is perfect. When the nori's reduced to a powder, add twice as much salt and an eighth of a teaspoon of celery seeds, if you have them. Blend again. Sprinkle on everything.

Perhaps the most well-known source of umami in Australia is a salty black paste in a squat jar. First made over ninety years ago in Port Melbourne, Vegemite is one of our food products known around the world. In global gastronomic circles, Vegemite is recognised as Australia's source of umami alongside Germany's sauerkraut, Italy's parmesan cheese, Malaysia's shrimp paste belachan, Thailand's fish sauce and Spain's anchovies.

Like Holden cars, Aeroplane Jelly and Chiko Rolls, Vegemite is one of our greatest and most iconic brands. Sold as a healthy spread to smear on our toast, its 1950s radio advertising jingle 'We're Happy Little Vegemites' was absorbed into our national vernacular. It was championed as our globally recognised condiment in Men At Work's 1981 song 'Down Under', in which Colin Hay buys bread from a muscular 6-foot-4 Brusselaar and asks if he speaks his language. In return he gets a smile and a Vegemite sandwich.

And just like Holden cars, Aeroplane Jelly and Chiko Rolls, Vegemite is American. It is owned by Kraft Australia, itself a wholly owned subsidiary of Mondelēz, where it sits alongside brands such as Toblerone, Philadelphia Cream Cheese and Oreos.

The Vegemite recipe was developed by a food chemist called Cyril Callister at Fred Walker's eponymous cheese factory in Albert Park. Walker was in debt to the tune of £80,000 from a previous failed business venture and was developing new food lines to push himself back in the black. He was working on a formula to make a paste from the yeast left over from the brewing process.

This was not a new concept. The process of extracting the nutritious insides of yeast cells had been developed in Germany in the previous century. The English had already developed Marmite, a yeast extract first produced in 1902 in Burton on Trent using post-ferment brewer's yeast from the nearby Bass Brewery, thus solving the problem of what to do with spent yeast.

The food culture of creating concentrated nutritious extracts packed in tins and jars extended even further back, to the Franco-Prussian War, when Scottish-born Canadian John Lawson Johnston developed Johnston's Fluid Beef to feed Napoleon III's Army. It was later renamed Bovril. This was made by boiling down beef in abattoirs in Brazil.

Callister's Australian version of a yeast extract was developed in 1923 with marketing beginning the following year. The name Vegemite was supposedly chosen at random from competition entries pulled from a hat by Walker's daughters. The winners were local Albert Park girls whose entry mirrored the marketing phrase on the first amber-coloured jars: 'Pure Vegetable Extract' and 'delicious on sandwiches and toast. Improves the flavour of soups, stews and gravies'.

In 1926 Walker formed a new company with James L Kraft of Chicago, called The Kraft Walker Cheese Co., to process cheese. By 1930 manufacturing for both companies was consolidated, and when Walker died of hypertensive heart disease in 1935, the Australian holdings of the company were absorbed by Kraft in Chicago.

The Vegemite plant is now in Salmon Street, Port Melbourne. You may never have seen it, but anyone driving to Melbourne Airport from the city surely would have smelled it. Vegemite is made from post-ferment brewer's yeast trucked in from breweries around Melbourne and, during processing of the yeast, releases a sweet bakery-like aroma into the air. The yeast is treated with plant enzymes to break down its cell walls to leave, basically, a lot of protein, B vitamins and amino acids that are cooked with salts and natural vegetable flavours, including onion-seed extract and celery-seed extract. For several months after, the 'black velvet' is stored in drums to mature. Freshly made Vegemite and Vegemite that has been stored for a few months are very different, as it takes time for the flavour to develop. The Vegemite is heated, extruded into jars and sealed. More than 25 million jars are produced annually, with 95 per cent sold in Australia and New Zealand.

Vegemite's appeal is deep-rooted in our brains. Its saltiness pleases our ancient and instinctive desire for salt, while the amino acids give an enticing, mouth-filling sense of umami. However, its intensity means that it is an acquired taste.

And it is because Vegemite is an acquired taste that we are so fond of it and so defensive of it. As Australians, we take great delight in watching the facial reactions of people from other cultures when they taste Vegemite for the first time. The question 'Have you tasted Vegemite?' has replaced 'What do you think of Australia?' in celebrity interviews.

In 2006 Australian officials investigated reports that the US Food and Drug Administration had banned sales of Vegemite because of its levels of folate, an additive regulated in the United States. The Australian Embassy was aware of reports that people were being stopped from bringing the breakfast spread into the United States. The story later turned out to be based on rumour.

Transpacific relations were further tested in 2011, when Prime Minister Julia Gillard was at a school in the United States, meeting President Obama. She was asked by a student: 'What is Vegemite?' and replied: 'Right. This is a bit of a difference between the President and I. I love Vegemite.' Obama replied, with a laugh: 'It's horrible! … it's like a quasi-vegetable byproduct paste that you smear on your toast for break-fast. Sounds good, doesn't it?' The reason we love Vegemite is because others hate it. It helps define who we are.

NOSE KNOWS BEST

Andrew Wood is a peasant. He is a modern peasant. For him the call of the land was so great he turned his back on a career in publishing and bought a block of free-draining granite country near Heathcote and planted heritage vegetables. Wood was previously a pioneer in food niche marketing, publishing what many argue was Australia's best food and wine magazine at the tail end of the twentieth century and the beginning of the new one. It was called *Divine Food and Wine* and, at a time when the glossies were publishing recipes for lamb shanks and sticky date pudding, he was publishing several-thousand-word pieces on Australian cheese and wild yeast wines.

The first time I saw Wood was back in the 1990s. He was a guest speaker at the Royal Melbourne Institute of Technology, where I was studying professional writing and editing. Back then, he admitted that he mortgaged his house several times to finance his magazine. Wood gave me my first break at writing long-form stories, paying twenty cents a word (a rate that some publishers twenty years on think is reasonable reward). In the early 2000s I was lucky enough to organise a massive lamb tasting in which we collected ten different rare-breed lamb carcasses from across the state and had them butchered in an inner-city restaurant. Each of the ten beasts was served five different ways, so the tasters could get an understanding of the ways the different cuts of lamb tasted: meat from the forequarter, ribs, rump, leg and shank. The tasters came from the realms of the food and wine world and each consumed roughly 20 to 50 grams in each tasting. This meant that at the end of the session they would have consumed between one to two-and-a-half kilograms of lamb. One of the tasters, an up-and-coming chef called Andrew McConnell from a little restaurant called Diningroom 211, claimed, albeit jokingly, that he was traumatised by the event.

Divine was marginal, to say the least, and Wood was decades ahead of the game. When the digital age spread across the planet, one of the world's best food and wine magazines quietly folded.

The next time I saw Wood was at my local farmers' market. Very quietly he and his business partner, Jill McCalman, had packed up, moved out bush and turned into peasants. They came to town with their ute loaded up, like Okies. In the back of their HiLux were crates of leafy greens, root vegetables and tomatoes. Tomatoes with names so exotic they sounded like they were titles from a swamp boogie songbook. Rouge de Marmande. Glenora Green. Black from Tula. They were green, burgundy, yellow and campfire red. They were every colour other than the fire-engine red of the Roma tomatoes most farmers were growing. 'I put my money where my mouth was,' said Wood. He had always been a critic of food that lacked natural flavour. In his careers as an editor and publisher he had favoured chefs who had gone out on a limb and sought out natural flavoursome ingredients.

He held a red tomato flushed with yellow in one hand and a sharp, stubby knife in the other. He pushed the sharp blade into the thin skin and easily carved out a fat wedge. The skin was fine and the flesh soft and strongly aromatic of … well, tomato. The jelly-like pulp within the flesh held fat seeds. I placed the tomato on my tongue. It was delicious. Nicely sharp, a touch sweet and a lovely mouth-filling savoury sensation. The tomato was named by an American farmer in the nineteenth century for its meaty flesh. Its name was Beefsteak. It was a variety of heritage tomato selected for flavour.

Wood and McCalman specialise in heritage vegetables, and called their business Glenora Heritage Produce. 'We have tried many varieties of heirloom vegetables and failed,' said McCalman. 'Now we have our tried-and-tested varieties but they are still a bugger to get perfect.' She explained that heritage tomatoes were bred for certain growing conditions and not commercial yields.

Heritage vegetables represent the choice of varieties of fruit and vegetables that were available to growers prior to the rationalisation of agriculture that started after World War I and gathered pace after World War II. These were vegetables that were bred to grow in certain climates. So, a bean bred to ripen in upstate New York might not set seed in the hot, dry summer of Central Victoria. But when they do find conditions to be agreeable, heritage vegetables grow in such a way that they produce complex aromas and depth of flavour.

To prove the point, Wood offered me a piece of carrot. It was sweet. And incredibly 'carroty' would be the only way to describe it. The vegetables he offered were all likewise intensely flavoured. 'What we have today is a dearth of flavour in the vegetables most people buy on a day-to-day basis. Here, in front of you, these vegetables are grown for one thing and one thing only, and that is flavour,' he said with a passionate rising intonation. 'The vegetables grown for the supermarket are grown for one thing. And that is shareholder profit. They have to look good for the longest time possible while being handled by pickers, packers, shelf stackers and customers,' he went on. 'They are not grown for flavour.'

Flavour is essential to health. The scientific links have been established for over a decade. An article in *Science* magazine published in February 2006 stated that, as they grow, plants produce many different compounds, only some of which can be sensed by humans. 'Volatile profiles are defining elements of the distinct flavours of individual foods,' the article stated. 'Flavour volatiles are derived from an array of nutrients including amino acids, fatty acids and carotenoids.' The article mentioned that in tomatoes, for example, 'almost all of the important flavour related volatiles are derived from essential nutrients. The predominance of volatiles derived from essential nutrients and health promoting compounds suggest that these volatiles provide important information about the nutritional makeup of food.'

So while our tongue is hardwired to detect the presence of protein, salt, energy and danger, our olfactory system—our ability to smell—is hardwired to detect compounds that we find attractive that are beneficial to us. It is no wonder that we can detect carotenoids—these are the compounds that give yellow and orange colour to vegetables. They are also incredibly good for us. The more agreeable flavour and aroma fresh food has, the better it is for us.

I spent the rest of the morning wandering the market. There were baby beetroots that smelled of raspberries, apples that smelled like honey, plums that reminded me of roses, lettuce that tasted milky. In my mind I was back in my childhood vegetable garden.

I returned to Andrew Wood and Jill McCalman. They were refilling their display boxes with fresh vegetables from their ute. They now sell to a handful of enlightened chefs in Melbourne, like Matt Wilkinson, who share their philosophy and understand why humans react so positively to quality flavours. Those restaurateurs are some of the most successful in the business and are happy to pay the premium Wood and McCalman ask for their vegetables.

It is interesting to note that, compared with our sense of taste, which is hardwired to our brain stem, our sense of smell goes through a completely different channel. Chemical compounds activate sensors in our nose that relay information to the brain. Those aromas are laid down in a format similar to the way we remember vision. Not the exact aroma but a representation of it. Those aroma images are stored in the same part of the brain in which we experience emotion. It is no wonder, then, that when one smells an old-fashioned rose, or a fragrant tomato, one is reminded of one's grandmother, with a particular yearning for the past.

9

Summer Bounty

The end of summer came so quickly. Our few tomato plants in our pocket-handkerchief-sized backyard had set good fruit but not enough to make tomato sauce. Every year for the past several decades we made sugo, or passata. When we bought our house, our first, a Victorian terrace, we decided to follow the examples of our Italian and Greek neighbours and plant a 'wog' garden. We felt we had to. The week after we signed the mortgage papers, the Lehman Brothers collapse signalled the official beginning of the GFC.

It was explained to me when I first arrived in the city from the country, way back in the mid-1980s, that 'wogs' owned their houses faster than 'skips' because they could feed themselves from the backyard. 'Wog' was originally a derogatory name for post-World War II migrants, but was appropriated by the community and by the late eighties was worn as a badge of pride. At the same time, the term 'skip' was coined, the cultural Yin to the wog Yang. 'Skip' is the pejorative term given to Anglos by 'wogs', the term an abbreviation of *Skippy the Bush Kangaroo*. This was a television show about a treacherous national park on the outskirts of Sydney, in which each episode a guest character or one of the central cast would find themselves on the edge of a dangerous precipice, bitten by a snake or unexpectedly lost. They could only be saved by the intervention of a sentient kangaroo called Skippy, who could communicate by clicking and pointing. It was the *Game of Thrones* of its day.

So, having been labelled a skip by my wog mates, I felt it was only natural that the first garden I owned (with my partner and the bank) would be a wog garden. This meant squeezing an olive, lemon and bay tree into the frontyard and growing herbs between them. We planted over thirty food trees on our tiny block of land, underplanting them with perennial herbs and self-seeding bitter greens. The north-facing strip of concrete was covered in planters and filled with annual herbs, corn, beans, zucchini and tomatoes. The one factor I hadn't taken into account was the possums. They love tomatoes.

Determined to still make our passata and sugo, I drove up to the hills to my mates' place—Meagan Bertram and Steve Briggs at Yarra Valley Gourmet Greenhouse, who grow the most amazing tomatoes for restaurants. Many are heritage-breed tomatoes and as much as I love them, they are temperamental compared with modern hybrids. Which means there are always a lot of seconds. This was good for me as I was able to get several boxes to make my sauces. The downside was that they were not all red tomatoes. In fact, most were yellow- and orange-coloured tomatoes.

Back home we washed the tomatoes, and ran them through our 1-horsepower Tre Spade tomato mill. I own it together with my neighbour. In autumn it makes passata and in winter we used it to make sausages. We crushed the tomatoes and poured the juice into big wide pots and cooked the juice down to reduce it by half. We poured the passata into Fowlers Vacola jars. These are Australian-made jars with wide mouths used for preserving fruit My Italian neighbours use old beer bottles and crown seals for their passata. I like the mix of Anglo and Italian, of the Fowlers Vacola and sugo. It's that hybrid bastardry of Australian culture that I love. We come from everywhere and we can be whoever we want to be. I am a self-appointed skippy wog. A 'skog'. Or is that 'wippy'? Restaurateur Guy Grossi coined a magnificent phrase that describes the wog culture in Victoria. He calls himself and his like 'Melbournese', as in Milanese.

Here are some notes from our garden and kitchen over that first summer and autumn.

MAKING THE MOST OF SUMMER PRODUCE

Beans

We made bean rockets out of some 2-metre-long tea-tree sticks a neighbour had thrown out in hard rubbish. We planted three of these in small plots of turned-over soil and joined them up like the skeleton of a teepee. We planted climbing beans at the base of the poles and watched them wind their way up. The beans bloomed with cascades of glorious red flowers, which were soon swarming with bees. The flowers quickly withered to reveal tiny beans. Tiny beans taste like large ones but are more intense. Beans ripen in flush, creating a sudden glut. It is a good idea to pick some beans earlier than others, to slow down this bounty. Beans sliced very fine, either lengthways or on the bias, can be served in a piled salad with small pieces of ricotta, mint and parsley, dressed with a vinaigrette and dusted with ground nuts and cumin. Steamed beans are delicious with a handful of sourdough breadcrumbs that have been fried in a few tablespoons of extra virgin olive oil and a few cloves of crushed garlic. Fresh beans cooked with tomato passata and onions, and served with loads of fresh parsley, pass muster with kids.

Carrots

I am one of those old-fashioned (mean) fathers who doesn't buy my children anything other than clothes and books as presents, and when we go shopping only allows them to buy a treat at the greengrocer. By the age of seven, my youngest could read the nutrition panel on food. She pointed out that Nutri-Grain has just on 30 grams of sugar per 100 grams. My oldest daughter said that makes Nutri-Grain 32 per cent sugar. My daughters are also allowed to buy whatever seeds they like. My youngest, unbeknownst to me, planted carrots all around the garden in early spring. Come summer I was weeding out baby carrots. No bigger than your thumb, after careful washing these tiny carrots can be added whole to a salad. Fresh, small carrots only need warming in butter.

Just prior to serving, fold through a few tablespoons of finely chopped dill, mint or parsley. A simple vegetable peeler, taken to a carrot, creates lots of shreds of carrots that can be folded with crushed roasted nuts, feta cheese and chopped parsley. Grated carrot can give some sweetness and richness to pasta sauce. Grated carrot, when sautéed gently in butter or oil, can also be added to grain and pulse dishes.

Corn

I planted the corn in patches. Squares of corn surrounded by lawn. I watched the little spikes of green emerge from the earth in spring and unfurl their leaves, setting their cobs and flower head on top. Growing corn reminds me of the *M.A.S.H.* episode in which Father Mulcahy plants a vegetable garden. Over the season, tragedies come and go but throughout, he tends carefully to that garden of corn. Come summer he harvests the corn and gives the cobs to the cook, Igor. The cast talks eagerly of chewing corn kernels right off the cob, dreaming of melted butter oozing down their chins. When Igor reveals he has cooked the fresh cobs into gluggy army-style creamed corn, Father Mulcahy loses his priestly cool.

Fresh corn, picked young, needs very little done to it, as the skin on the kernels is quite fine and the inside quite creamy. Steaming for a few minutes is good. I prefer grilling by laying the cobs, husk on, over a very low flame or coals. When corn gets older, the skin on the kernel toughens and the interior becomes harder and more starchy. Older cobs need a little more cooking. With older cobs I gently peel down the outer leaves one by one to reveal the kernels. These are given a good rub with garlic-infused extra virgin olive oil, or butter, and a little salt; then the leaves of the husk are replaced and tied in place with 'string' made from torn strips of husk. After this the cobs are grilled as per usual. Corn kernels sautéed in butter with softened onions until hot and folded through a warm wild rice salad with parsley are delicious. Remember: corn loves butter.

Cucumbers

A freshly harvested cucumber is crisp and crunchy like an apple. A little dish we learned from a bistro in Hong Kong was roughly sliced pieces of cucumber with a dressing of lemon juice, sesame oil and soy sauce, and topped with toasted sesame seeds. Long strips or juliennes of cucumber can be served like vegetable spaghetti, with a little salt and finely crushed garlic, finished with a simple splash of extra virgin olive oil and balsamic vinegar. Julienned cucumber mixed through coleslaw makes it lighter to eat. Cucumber, dill and yoghurt goes with almost everything.

Potatoes

We grew our potatoes in a hessian sack. We bought the sack at a stockfeed store in the inner suburbs that once sold chaff and hay to pre-automobile horses. Started in 1888, Murphy Brothers in Hawthorn sold stockfeed mainly to horses but also to milk-producing cows and goats. In the days before refrigeration, milking cows and nanny goats were commonplace in large suburban gardens. The billy, or male, goats were often harnessed to small jinker-like carts and used for children's entertainment and also transport. Hence the term 'billycart'. The things you learn from people in feedstores.

We tightly packed the hessian sack with straw, then laid down a thick layer of compost, some sprouting potatoes, more compost and more straw. It was basically a sack full of leaves until the end of summer, when the potatoes started flowering. There is a technique for harvesting potatoes without pulling out the entire plant, called 'bandicooting'. This entails running your hands into the straw or soil under the dripline of the plant, or where the rain drips onto the ground on the outside edge of the plant. Here one can find immature potatoes that can be twisted away from the roots without damaging the plant or affecting the other potatoes. This means one can harvest tiny little potatoes. Which are delicious deep-fried and served with aioli. Young potatoes are brilliant for potato salad. I still love adding a mix of finely chopped white onions, olive oil, vinegar, sugar, salt, pepper and a stock cube to a bowl of very hot, freshly boiled baby potatoes and letting the dressing soak in. This was a recipe taught to me by an old German couple when I was growing up. Another tasty way of serving potato salad is with quark, finely chopped mint and parsley, a little sherry vinegar and a pinch of salt. Mashed potato pureed with loads of butter and cheese, using a stick blender, becomes a rich, sticky mate to ratatouille. Chickpeas and potatoes make a great soup, and an excellent stew, and when cooked chickpeas and potatoes are fried with onions they are incredibly delicious. Grated potato, after being squeezed in a tea towel to remove juice, mixed with egg and parmesan, makes great galettes on which yummy things such as eggs or avocado can be served.

Zucchini

At the end of summer a joke is retold in the countryside in the southern states. Question: Why should you lock your car at night? Answer: So people don't fill it full of zucchinis. It almost sounds like one of those jokes that has been translated from a foreign language and has lost something along the way. But head to the countryside, where people are growing their own vegetables, and at the end of summer and the first months of autumn, zucchinis go berserk. A friend with small children said his son left his plastic tricycle next to a large zucchini. He swears that while he was sitting down having a beer after working in the garden, he saw the zucchini push over the trike. There was a *Star Trek* episode where the *Enterprise* was threatened by a truly adorable species of furry creatures called Tribbles. They were cute in every way possible except they reproduced like rabbits—seemingly on a mixture of Viagra and speed. The spaceship was literally overrun with these creatures. Zucchinis are the Tribbles of the vegetable world. They are quite clever too. When you pick a young zucchini, with all its buttery nuttiness and tiny soft seeds, you're sending an alarm signal to the plant. You have taken away its way of reproducing; therefore it needs to make more seed, so it flowers more and creates more zucchinis. You can extrapolate from here.

A farmer I met recently in Campania, Italy, showed me the vegetables she was growing for the handmade *sott'olio*, which means preserved 'under oil'. She grew varieties of zucchini not dissimilar to the common garden variety found in many Australian backyards. Instead of harvesting them when they were young, plump and thin-skinned, she let them grow on a little longer. She wanted the flesh that surrounds the seeds to swell and thicken. She wanted the skin to thicken a little as well, for when she went to process the zucchini she only took the flesh and skin. The seeds went to the pigs or to grow next year's crop. As a result, the zucchini plant only grew a handful of large zucchini. To finish the *sott'olio* she would cut the zucchini in slices, salt them and allow them to dry for several days in the sun. Once this was done she would hand-pack them as tightly as she could in a jar and cover them with a blend of extra virgin olive and sunflower oils. This she would then simmer in water, just below boiling, for fifty minutes.

Male zucchini flowers can be picked and placed on a corn tortilla with some mozzarella and a little truffle paste. The tortilla is folded and grilled on the flat grill or one at a time in a heavy-based frying pan. The Mexicans call these *quesadillas con queso y flores de calabaza* Normally they would use some *huitlacoche*, which is a corn fungus. You can buy *huitlacoche* tinned but truffle paste is better. Fine zucchini fritters can be made by grating zucchini and laying it out on a tea towel, then squeezing out the water. Add feta, a little egg and mint, to form quite a wet mixture. Fry, drain and serve with yoghurt. Just when zucchini is ripe, so is eggplant and tomato—perfect to make ratatouille.

There is something universally human about nursing a bounty of fruit and vegetables from the orchard or garden. A single arm nursing durable vegetables on the hip. Two arms folded, nestling softer offerings close to the chest. These are gentle and beautiful images often captured by artists. Loading your arms up with a cornucopia of home-grown plants makes you feel good, not only about yourself but being able to provide delicious and nourishing meals for your family. I believe that we all have a stronger relationship with the land, its furrows and ploughs and its rich moist earth than we have with guns and spears.

10

So Long and Thanks for all the Fish

As a food writer I have always had a problem assessing the environmental and ethical issues surrounding commercial fishing. Most reporting about the fishing industry comes from second-hand information from global environmental bodies about how bad the world's fisheries are. Horror stories of poisonous Mekong prawn farms, aquatic dead zones under salmon farms caused by their faeces, and Dutch supertrawlers that hoover every living thing into their bowels. I feel there is a lot of latent xenophobia woven into the texture of these stories and feel instinctively that the nature of them is too simplistic.

Compared with land-based food production, it is difficult to witness what goes on in boats on the high seas. I had always been suspicious about the fishing industry after I witnessed some commercial fishermen take their catch to the processor, where the fresh flipping fish were quickly scaled, gutted and filleted. The fillets were packed in a box lined with plastic sheets. The box was closed, sealed and placed in the freezer. On the side of the box was printed 'Fresh Fish'. The person who ran the small plant said to me, 'We only freeze it for a few days. It's "fresh frozen". It's not like it's deep frozen.'

One evening I found myself on a small fishing boat on Port Phillip Bay. The fishermen—yes, an all-male crew—set the boat into the water on the other side of Corio Bay, on which they were to fish. I found out later that local Geelong residents had been slashing the tyres of the fishermen's trailers. This more remote spot was safer. I was heading out to do a story for the paper, my feet squeezed into the rubber wader, gingerly holding my camera above the spray coming from the bow.

Fisherman Sam Georgiou powered his fishing boat through the water. He was grinning as we rode across the choppy wake of another boat. 'I love this,' Georgiou shouted over the din of the motor. 'I am one of the men who puts the fish on your table. Fresh, local fish. And we love what we do.' At the time, Georgiou was also chairman of the Western Port and Port Phillip Professional Fishermen's Association. Hundreds of fishermen once worked in the bay, selling their catch from the jetties and piers to which they tethered their boats. Scores of little piers, each servicing the community. By the beginning of the twentieth century there were just a dozen or so full-time licensed operators still fishing the 1950 square kilometres of the bay on a regular basis. Visitors to Melbourne query about eating fish out of a waterway so close to a large population. The truth of the matter is that the bay is quite healthy. It retains much of its seagrass beds and coral reefs at the head, where the bay meets Bass Strait. The shipping industry, through blasting to deepen the channel, has caused damage to the heads, while dredging has unleashed some heavy metals. Tests done comparing fairy penguins in St Kilda to their cousins in Western Port Bay showed the city birds had higher levels of mercury in their bodies than their country cousins, who do the daily waddle up the beach at Phillip Island.

Georgiou was working with another boat to catch the fish. The water they were working is very shallow and only a few hundred metres from the farms along the coast on the Bellarine Peninsula. His deckhand, Chris Nicholson, took a smaller boat and cut a broad arc in the water, letting out a long, dark net behind him. This was a seine net. It had floats on the top and little weights on the bottom, and was hauled through the water back towards the shore. The two ends were drawn together to form a purse. Pelicans and gulls flew in to take part in the action, diving into the water and flying off with fish in their beaks. Back on Georgiou's boat there was an urgent call on the radio. A seal had come crashing through the net. The air was thick with Greek curses. By the time we reached the nets, the seal was inside. Cormorants and terns had joined the party. The seal rolled and snorted about on the surface, diving below and reappearing with a black bream in its mouth.

'He'll scare all the fish out and eat the rest,' said Georgiou.

The sun dropped behind the horizon, flooding the sky with pinks and mauves. Waders on and standing chest high in the warm water, Georgiou and his fishing partner, Angelo Xenos, sorted the fish. Measuring stick in one hand, they threw their fish into bins on board. Undersized fish went into the bay. 'I'll see you next year,' said Xenos to a little garfish. The catch was not great. Nicholson threw a single Moreton Bay bug onto the deck. 'When I was working with the scallop boats twenty years ago we used to see lots of these,' said Georgiou. 'But not so many these days. The bay is much cleaner than it was back then. Then there was so much more algae, now it is the sun-bleached seagrass that is the problem.'

A large flathead was landed, a slight discolouration on its head. 'Remember a few months back there was the lesions scare with the bay fish?' asked Xenos. 'That was due to the hot weather. Sunburned fish! Now they have recovered.'

The sorting went on. High-value fish, King George whiting, flathead and garfish were separated into different boxes. The team motored on in the dark further down the bay. They shot another net in the still water near Clifton Springs. A fat moon rose over the Bellarine Peninsula. There was a familiar snort. The seal had followed them. The catch was dismal. The men grabbed a quick bite to eat. Xenos opened a container filled with dried meats, olives, cheese and spanakopita, made by his wife that morning.

They headed back to shore to wash and sort their catch. Within the hour they would have dropped the fish off at the fish market. It was 2 a.m.

Georgiou looked into the boxes. 'Bloody seal,' he said. 'But you know what? There's nothing we can do. His kind have been here long before we got here. It's everybody's bay.'

That evening on the water taught me a lot about that style of fishing. It was a simple procedure that used technology that was thousands of years old. I have seen photographs of similar nets used by the Yuin Aboriginal people from the South Coast of New South Wales. The modern bay fishers have underwater fish finders and powerful little boats, but the rest of the technology is pretty simple. Port Phillip Bay is a relatively small fishery, with commercial fishers producing about 600 tonnes of fish annually; its real importance lies in the fact that it is so close to Melbourne. A fish caught in the bay in the early hours of the morning can well be on the dining table later that same night or the next day. Port Phillip Bay is a sustainable fishery and has been recognised as such by environmental bodies like Greenpeace. It is a model of how looking after waterways and the surrounding environment benefits everybody. It is perhaps one of the best sustainable fisheries in the world, producing quality fish that any ethical pescatarian would be pleased to eat. In November 2015 the Victorian Labor Government, supported by the Liberal opposition, voted to end commercial netting in Port Phillip Bay, to appease the recreational fishing lobby. It was a triumph of political expediency over old-fashioned common sense. In April 2016, when the bans came into place, I went to my local fish shop and where once had been glowing fresh squid and calamari and bay fish rigid with rigor mortis, there now sat two tired-looking factory farmed salmon from Tasmania.

Australians have always settled in places of great bounty. Scientist and author Tim Flannery has described the upper reaches of Port Phillip Bay at the time of settlement as being a 'temperate Kakadu'—wetlands teeming with 'brolgas, Cape Barren geese, swans, ducks, eels and frogs'. Great middens of native angasi oyster shells in the dunes along the beaches around Port Phillip Bay indicate where Bunurong and Wathaurong Aboriginal peoples sat down on the beach for Melbourne's original oyster frenzies. Back then the oysters gathered in big reefs ringing the bay. The feasts continued when the whitefellas arrived. During the gold rush, oysters dredged from the bay were served with French champagne chilled on ice shipped from America. Oyster shells, both those harvested from the bay and from historical middens, were also burned, to make lime for cement to hold together what are now our fine old buildings. In the gold rush era, Victorians' appetite for oysters was insatiable and by the 1880s, after Melburnians had eaten almost all the oysters in the bay, we began shipping them in from Tasmania. Within a few generations we had eaten out one of the great oyster waterways of the world. The feast continued all the way down Bass Strait and the east coast of Tasmania.

Flying in over its snow-capped highlands, you approach Hobart Airport over a clear estuary called Pittwater. It was here that the first Pacific oysters were brought to Australia, from Japan, in 1947. (Earlier plans, in the late 1930s, were stymied by World War II.) Most died. Later, spat, or tiny baby oysters, were flown in and the survival rate was much higher. Today, Tasmania produces around 2250 tonnes of Pacific oysters a year. An industry that is the result of an earlier environmental catastrophe.

In New South Wales some oyster growers consider the introduced Pacific oyster to be another environmental catastrophe. Pacific oysters are incredibly fast growing, taking just a year to eighteen months to reach maturity in the warm waters of New South Wales. A native Sydney rock oyster will take three to four years to reach maturity. This fast growth rate means that when Pacific oysters spawn, they colonise the rocks on which the native Sydney rock oysters grow and simply outgrow them. The Sydney rock oyster farmers depend on wild oyster spawn to repopulate their own farms, while Pacific oysters are almost exclusively grown from hatchery-raised spat. Breeders have successfully produced a Pacific oyster called a triploid that does not reproduce. This is being championed in New South Wales by some growers, who see it as a better environmental solution.

Oysters are the canaries of the food production system. They are sensitive little filter feeders and if any muck gets in the waterway, then they don't grow as well or will die. If the waterway is polluted, either by chemicals or sewage, the entire waterway will have to be closed down until the pollution ceases. In southern New South Wales there is a battle for resources. The logging industry wants the forests. The forests filter the water. The oyster industry wants clean water.

'Good oysters start with good water,' oyster farmer Shane Buckley told me. 'If you have good water, then you can grow good oysters.' He has a lease at Wapengo Lake, an estuary about forty-five minutes north of Merimbula on the New South Wales South Coast. He is a quiet man with a dry sense of humour and a real passion for what he does. He explained that oysters are filter feeders. They take in water and filter the plankton on which they feed. Whatever the plankton feed on helps influence the taste of the oyster. Trace minerals in the water also determine the flavour of an oyster. The saltier the water in which the oysters are grown, the more amino acids they produce, some of which produce umami.

We motored out onto the water in his aluminium punt. Buckley pointed to a mountain in the distance. 'That's Mumbulla. It's a mountain sacred to the local Aboriginal families and the headwaters of the Wapengo Creek that runs into the lake,' he said. It is also close to an actively logged forestry site. Buckley explained that a few years back, he and fellow oyster growers worked with the forestry industry to make sure run-off from logging sites didn't enter the waterway. They also worked with the local shire to tarmac the dirt road that runs along the side of the lake.

'But when the rains come there is always the threat of nasty bugs like E. coli washing into the water,' Buckley said. 'The bugs don't last long but the fishery is closed until tests done on the oysters come back negative. It's not a big problem for us like it is for people on more populated waterways.'

This is the same across the nation: health authorities monitor the water conditions in which oysters grow, to avoid outbreaks of disease. In 1997, after heavy rain, more than 400 people were infected with hepatitis A and one person died from eating oysters from Wallis Lake in New South Wales. The oysters had been contaminated with sewage overflowing from septic tanks.

Australians eat about 16 million dozen oysters annually. New South Wales produces the bulk of the crop, 41 per cent, with most of those being the native Sydney rock oyster. South Australia grows 37 per cent of our oysters, these being the Pacific oyster, originally from Japan. Tasmania grows almost all of the rest, mainly Pacifics, while Queensland has a small industry, south of Hervey Bay, growing rock oysters.

Buckley gently motored up to a line of plastic baskets suspended from a taut wire just above the water, being careful not to disturb the reed bed that had grown back since he removed the old-fashioned wooden rack system installed in the mid-twentieth century. The shade from the infrastructure killed the weed. He pushed the boat closer, like a gondolier. As the tide rose and fell, the baskets either floated upside-down or hung the right way up.

'This is what we call tumbling,' said Buckley. It helps the oyster grow a deeper shell and a fuller 'fish', as the flesh is referred to in the trade. This method, used extensively across the industry, encourages the growth of the muscle that closes the shell when the oyster is exposed to air—the adductor—but doesn't overwork it, giving the flesh a less chewy mouthfeel.

Nearby were what appeared to be venetian blinds floating in the water. They were in fact plastic slats on which the spat, or baby oysters, settle after they are fertilised. It's this urge to reproduce that determines so much of any oyster's quality. In spring and early summer the oysters fatten up and become laden with sperm and eggs. But then, when the water is warm enough and there is a downpour, the oysters pump the water full of eggs and sperm, which commingle in the water. The resulting spat eventually cling on to whatever surface they can find, from rock to unlucky hermit crab.

After spawning, oysters appear spent and flaccid, lose weight and that creamy taste and texture. Shortly, however, they regain some condition and have a more flinty taste, meatier texture and aromas of iodine, making them more suitable for eating with a dry white wine, such as muscadet or chablis. Oysters can spawn as long as the water is warm enough and there is a flow of fresh water. Their urge to spawn can be kicked on by a full moon as well.

When I asked Buckley about the adage 'never eat an oyster in a month without an R', he replied bluntly, 'What a lot of bullshit. I have a lot of French customers, who prefer them after they have spawned.'

Buckley will harvest these oysters when they are about three years old and sell them directly to restaurants. The one thing he insists on is that his oysters are freshly shucked—he won't sell them to restaurants that open oysters before service.

'What's the point?' he asked. 'I have gone to all this trouble to create the best oysters I can. Why let them sit open for a few hours? They are at their best the moment they are opened.' I mentioned to him that for me at that moment oysters were off the menu.

Buckley pointed to the sand dune on the other side of the estuary. There was a large rise in the sand covered by light scrub, banksias and wattles. 'That is a midden. They are all along the coast here. The Aboriginal people ate and still eat what the land had to offer,' he said. 'If you caught a goanna, you ate it. If there were daisy yams you dug them up and ate them. Look at all that food,' he said, pointing to the Sydney rock oysters that were growing on the rocks. 'I don't think I have ever heard of an Indigenous vegetarian.'

Seeing the way that Shane and other oyster growers look after not only the waterway but the hinterland gave me another ethical choice to think about when My Year Without Meat was eventually over.

11

The Denouement

There is a 1968 film about King Henry II called *The Lion in Winter* starring Peter O'Toole, Katharine Hepburn, Anthony Hopkins and John Castle. In it the old king, played by O'Toole, discovers he is being usurped by his sons, played by Hopkins and Castle. He throws them both into the dungeon to await their death. Down there they hear him coming. Prince Richard, played by Hopkins, says, 'He's here. He'll get no satisfaction out of me. He isn't going to see me beg,' to which Castle's Prince Geoffrey replies derisively, 'My, you chivalric fool … as if the way one fell down mattered.' Hopkins draws himself up and responds calmly, 'When the fall is all there is, it matters.'

THE DEATH

We keep reserves of energy in our body stored in different ways. Some of it is stored as muscle sugar. When you exert yourself, like when lifting a weight or climbing a hill, the sugar in your muscles, called glycogen, is combined with oxygen to power muscles. When there is not enough oxygen to react with the glycogen, a compound called lactate forms. It causes the pH in your muscles to change and momentarily you feel a burning sensation. When you get your breath back a little, the lactate changes back to another substance, called pyruvate, which reacts with oxygen to create energy. Things go back to normal.

That muscle sugar, glycogen, is an important part of the enjoyment people get from eating meat. When an animal dies the glycogen is transformed into lactic acid. Because the animal is dead there is no oxygen pumping around the blood. So an anaerobic transformation occurs, where enzymes break down the glycogen into lactic acid. This lowers the pH. The lower the pH of something, the more acidic it is. Lactic acid gives the meat a clean finish on the palate. It also assists in the dry ageing of meat. This is the process in which a whole carcass, or part thereof, is hung in a coolroom and allowed to age for anywhere from fourteen days to three months. During this period the skin and fat protect the meat inside from the air, stopping it from drying out and mummifying. It protects the meat from bugs getting inside and spoiling it. The lower pH also helps stop the growth of the bugs.

The other part of dry ageing is that enzymes break down the muscles, making them more tender. Enzymes also break down proteins into amino acids. As we know, amino acids, such as glutamate, make food taste yummier. Ever noticed how different a chicken tastes when it is close to (but not past) its use-by date? Try it. Even an extra few days in the fridge will increase the flavour of your average chook.

This is how marinades work. These are often high-acid preparations, in which we immerse meat to add flavour and tenderise the flesh. Some acids denature animal protein. Add lemon juice to raw fish and you get the classic dish ceviche. Put pineapple with meat and the lot can quickly turn to mush as the enzyme bromelase breaks down the muscle fibre. There is another element to marinating and that is time. These acidic environments slow down bugs that would otherwise make meat go off. By allowing the meat to age, marinades retard bacterial decomposition and enhance enzymatic breakdown. Giving meat a good marination not only allows it to take on the flavour of the herbs and juices around it but also develop more naturally occurring deliciousness from amino acids. Traditional dishes like escabeche, in which game meats and fish are immersed in spiced vinegar, were very, very acidic and were more of a pre-refrigeration preservative than a marinade. Despite the meat being quite sour, escabeche is very delicious, as the protein inside is quietly breaking down into amino acids.

The takeout from this is that when an animal is slaughtered, you want as much glycogen as possible to remain in its muscles. You want the muscle sugar left in the muscles so it can be turned into lactic acid. This is something that good stockmen know instinctively.

TWO DEATHS

Celebrity US farmer Joel Salatin talks about his animals having fulfilling lives with plenty of feed and plenty of other animals to hang around with. Then they have 'just one bad day'. Their slaughter day. For much of my life I thought the death of the animals we eat was instant and painless. When I was young, about ten years old, there was a bloke called Roy Judd who used to visit the family farm. He was a butcher. He was also the slaughterman. We would choose an animal from the herd of cattle we raised on the bush blocks out the back of the farm. We would cross a Hereford bull over a Friesian cow. A small group of cattle were sequestered away from the main herd and kept in a paddock near the large machinery shed. Roy used to say, 'Lonely cows don't make for good eating.' They were given an extra feed of hay each day around mid-morning, as Roy liked to go fishing early in the morning. The cattle would gather around the hay and quietly chew their way through the pile, one of the older girls occasionally swiping another, giving a firm nudge with the side of her head. Roy would come in his car and set up his block and tackle, lay out his knives and saws, and prepare great tubs for guts and buckets for blood. He kept his gun wrapped in a towel. A twenty-two rifle. The Australian farmer's gun of choice for dispatching vermin and injured animals. It was old but it was clean. A bit like Roy, I used to think. He was always neatly presented for the job he was about to do. English born, he had that skin that turned honey coloured in the summer sun. He was polite and quite funny, but mostly he had a reassuring calmness about him. The type of bloke you could rely on in times of trouble.

We would wander over to a post under the shade of a large pine tree by the cattle, the gun pointing down by his side, its silhouette masked by his body. He didn't want the animals to find any cause for alarm. He rested the barrel on the post and looked down its sight. He whistled once. The cows looked up. There was a loud crack in the mid-morning air, the cows scattered and ran. Except one. She became rigid for a second. If a cow can look dismayed, then that's how she appeared. Suddenly her head went down and her legs stiffened and seemed to shake. Roy put the safety catch on his gun and deftly opened the gate, pulled out a knife and cut open the arteries in her neck. Bright red blood frothed and flowed out onto the deep green of the pasture. That is the speed and surprise that every slaughterman strives for. If slaughter were ever to be considered humane, this is a contender to be the definitive way.

THE FRENCH SLAUGHTERMEN

The firing squad is a method of execution mostly reserved for military punishments and, until recently, an alternative to the ballot box in many South American countries. It is the duty of every member of a firing squad to fire their gun. They are to take aim and fire at the prisoner's heart. The squad is told, however, that one or more of them has a gun loaded with a blank bullet. This means that none of the men who felt the kick in their shoulder as their gun discharged was able to know for sure which of them fired the fatal round.

Humans have interesting ways of dealing with the abrogation of responsibility when it comes to taking a life. In ancient Greece there was a ceremonial sacrifice called Buphonia. In it, oxen were taken to the highest point of the Acropolis, where grain was laid in front of them by a member of one of the founding families. The first ox to step forward was considered to have offered itself up for sacrifice. A member of another one of the founding families then came forward and slayed the animal with an axe, before flinging away the axe and fleeing the scene of the crime.

A crime because, at the time, killing a working ox was a crime. They were essential for the economy. The ancient Greeks had a very clever way of handling this. A trial was held and the axe sharpeners were called up to explain their complicity in the murder. How could they have killed the ox? All they did was sharpen the blade. The water bearers then came forward and denied their responsibility. How could they have killed the ox? All they did was lustrate, or ceremoniously wash, the blade to purify it for the sacrifice. The axe bearer was then asked to defend himself. How could he have killed the ox? It was the axe that caused the contusion and bleeding. So, after they all declared their innocence, the axe was finally called up and tried for the murder. It was found guilty. And then exonerated! In some other circumstances, when a knife was used, the guilty knife was thrown out to sea. So the sacrifice was made, the Gods were appeased, the axeman went without punishment, a feast ensued and life went on.

Meat eaters have a similar system of complicity. This is how we are able to live with the reality that what is lying on a polystyrene tray was once a living animal. It is a tribal complicity where no one person takes responsibility for the taking of an animal's life. We didn't kill the cow. All we did was pay the butcher. The butcher didn't kill the cow, all he did was cut it up. The deliveryman didn't kill the cow. All he did was load it up from the abattoir. (To add another layer of disconnection, many of us now do not even pay a human. We pass a polystyrene tray over a barcode reader in a supermarket and put our coins or cards into a machine that seems pre-programmed to randomly say 'unexpected item in bagging area'.) If we handle meat with tongs when we cook it, the first part of our body to touch the flesh could be our teeth or lips. We take no responsibility for the death of the animal and are completely disconnected from its life.

The French have a way with words. They used to call slaughterhouses *tueries*. This roughly translates as 'massacre'. *Tuerie de masse* refers to a mass killing or a single act of genocide. *Tueries* were houses of mass killing. The French now call their slaughterhouses abattoirs. The word comes from the verb *abattre*, which means to 'bring down that which is standing'. An *abatteur* is both a slaughterman and a woodcutter.

The French are proud of the logic of death they brought to the slaughterhouse. It is arranged a bit like a Greek sacrifice where no one is responsible for killing the animal. Here one person stuns the animal. The other bleeds it. To stun and to bleed, *assommer et saigner*. When one *abatteur* gives a blow to an animal's head with a blunt instrument, he delivers it to the other *abatteur* in the manner of '*il est comme mort*—it is as if dead'. It doesn't matter what the man who bleeds the animal does because it's not going to live after a blow like that but the man who delivers the stunning blow didn't kill the animal. There's a neatly crafted complicity in the murder of the animal, where no one takes responsibility. Which for those involved is perhaps a good thing. Killing for a living can be wearing on the soul.

Our relationship with animals has been defined by the premise that animals are not sentient. It has been as fundamental as the presumption of innocence. But that foundation principle of our society—that animals don't have emotions or fish don't feel pain—is slowly being eroded. Scientists are digitally dissecting live animals using magnetic resonance imaging and they are telling us that lobsters do have pain receptors and that cattle do experience fear. These studies bring into question the very tenet on which we allow ourselves to eat meat.

Livestock use up a lot of their energy stores when their fight or flight instinct kicks in. If an animal is stressed or experiences fear shortly prior to slaughter, it metabolises its glycogen, its muscle sugar. With the muscle sugar gone the meat doesn't drop in pH and you end up with what is known in the industry as dark cutting meat. This is why the quality end of the meat industry has instituted some back-to-basics animal husbandry to try to achieve premium quality beef.

Peter Greenham from HW Greenham and Sons is a sixth-generation beef business operator from the western suburbs of Victoria. A few years back he and his family started working with Sydney restaurateur Neil Perry to develop a premium line of beef that was slightly older than the normal young cattle slaughtered for the domestic market, with more developed flavoured flesh and completely grass fed. The Greenhams bought the Blue Ribbon abattoir in Smithton in the Circular Head region of north-west Tasmania. There the rainfall reaches around a metre a year and two metres in the hinterland hills, much of which is covered by the Tarkine cool-temperate rainforest. They have a network of around 600 small family farms from whom they buy their cattle. Around there they still raise the old-fashioned Angus, short black stock that were bred to do well on the rolling hills of Aberdeenshire. Which, like Circular Head, is green, wet and often cold. The farmers also raise the English beef breed Hereford, considered by many aficionados to be the king of the beef breeds when it comes to flavour. Head to the feedlots and you'll find bigger-framed black Angus. The modern Angus look very different from the animals of the same name sixty years ago. Angus were smaller, shorter-legged animals. Modern Angus are often infused with the genetics of the larger-framed European cattle—big frames from which to hang more meat. Greenham, however, likes his animals shorter, stockier and older. If, like most Australians, you're eating beef from the supermarket, it is probably no more than a year old. That is after sexual maturity, but the animal is still not fully physically developed. Greenham likes his beasts twice as old again, sometimes around two and a half years. That's a lot of time and feed invested for not a lot of extra weight.

Greenham's strategy was to create a brand that delivered superior flavour gained from slaughtering more mature cattle. The brand would offer a guarantee of grass-fed beef, and aim to fulfil all the requirements that fussy foodies would be looking for.

Peter Greenham said, 'We have a never, ever policy on hormone growth promotants and antibiotics—both therapeutic and sub-therapeutic.' He was referring to the practice of using antibiotics. It's the meat industry's dirty little secret. Sub-therapeutic use of antibiotics means that they are given to animals not to treat illness, but to prevent it. Animals living in close proximity, in feedlots, chicken sheds or close-quarter pig sheds, are fed antibiotics. Not because they are sick, but because they might get sick. It is one of the reasons we humans are losing the fight against infection. Bugs are so exposed to antibiotics on a day-to-day basis in the places we raise animals for meat that they have gained resistance to antibiotics.

Forty per cent of the animals that enter the system Greenham's promotes don't end up with the company's Cape Grim label. They can be rejected in the paddock, in the yards at the abattoir or as they are hanging from a hook in the coolroom.

One of the reasons a carcass would be rejected is stress-induced dark cutting meat. To reduce the stress on the animals, almost all the herds are on farms less than an hour from the abattoir, which means they don't spend hours or days on a truck. The trucks are single layered as opposed to the larger-capacity two-storey trucks. Herds are kept together and the flooring in the yards is made of a soft, energy-absorbing material. Some of the farmers who grow animals for Greenham's export programme, which ships to Whole Foods in the United States, have signed up to the Global Animal Partnership, which sees greater emphasis on farm animal welfare such as banning the routine use of cattle prods, and following breeding programmes that do not affect the welfare of the animals. The Greenhams are respected in the business and in the paddock, in the butcher shop and by restaurateurs. They are known to pay 10 to 20 per cent more to farmers than others in the beef game do. Their Cape Grim brand has been recognised as one of the best commercial-scale beef brands in the nation.

EVERY BIRTH, EVERY DEATH, IS DIFFERENT

No animal wants to die. We are all hardwired for survival. In an abattoir, animals are trucked in and unloaded. There they are generally left with shelter and water, sometimes not shelter, for twenty-four hours to purge themselves—shit themselves out. They are herded to the door of the abattoir, which opens and lets one in at a time. There is the kill box. The animal is in a small space and cannot move. One slaughterman administers a blow from a bolt gun that stuns the animal—those who have seen the film *No Country for Old Men* might recall Javier Bardem's Chigurh and the creepy catch phrase he uses on unsuspecting humans: 'Would you hold still, please, sir?' Another slaughterman cuts the animal's neck to let it bleed out.

They say animals smell fear. I have watched cattle slaughtered at an abattoir. I have never seen a cow go into the kill box willingly. They need to be goaded and forced. Is it the blood or adrenalin they smell? Either way, they snort, and mucus sprays and swings from the nostrils, their legs splay as they try to get purchase with their hooves. Their eyes roll back in their head as the slaughterman approaches with the bolt gun. There's a 'whack' and the animal is rendered senseless, and the transformation from live animal to meat-in-a tray starts, a lethal reverse transubstantiation from body of life into meaty host.

12

The Elephant in the Room

It was one of those blowy Melbourne days when the wind swings to the north and promises warmer weather, bringing with it lungfuls of pollen and dust from up north. The location was a food festival held in a park and I was there to hear about a 'green meat' initiative, being spruiked by Meat and Livestock Australia (MLA). The emcee, an enthusiastic and professional young woman, was describing the important work cattle farmers had done in the Landcare movement, by fencing off native bush, replanting the land along waterways with native bush, creating shelter for cattle, and creating a better, healthier and more attractive environment for the cattle, native fauna and farmers. Then the emcee used the word 'happy' to describe the livestock. 'Happy'.

This struck me as an unusual use of anthropomorphism. It is a tactic used by animal rights activists to connect people to animals so they won't eat meat. By giving animals emotions, the MLA was playing a risky card. Happy cows means sentient cows.

Later, a west coast chef and farmer, Steve Earl, stood up to talk about his new business model of growing rose veal. Veal is from very young calves. Rose veal is from young cattle that are no longer calves but not yet sexually mature. His plan was to inseminate dairy cattle with semen from a beef breed and raise the offspring for several months before sending them off to slaughter. By creating a market for this rose veal, or 'pale beef', he would get a better return for the farmer. The other bonus was that no one would have to kill baby calves.

'Most male dairy calves are slaughtered within a few days of being born,' Earl said. 'Farmers don't get much for them. Calves are an essential part of the dairy industry, as a cow needs to calve to produce milk.'

What happened next was astonishing. Earl was taken aside by a representative of the MLA and told in no uncertain terms that cattle are not 'slaughtered'. The prescribed word he was to use in public was 'processed'. 'I was quite rattled,' said Earl afterwards. He was also told not to use the word 'product' but 'meat'. 'It felt like they were having a bet both ways.'

The avoidance of the word 'slaughter' but the promotion of a 'happy' life is the foundation lie on which the meat industry exists. For meat to exist, an animal has to die. This is a weakness at the heart of the meat industry that they are struggling to deal with. Death is not something that business is good at marketing.

THE PiG FARMERS

One of the new breed of pig farmers who uses the word 'happy' is Lauren Mathers. When I first met Mathers, she and her husband, Lachlan, had just embarked on a new life as pig farmers. They showed me with pride their herd of Berkshire sows snorting and grazing on the river flats near the Murray River at Barham in south-west New South Wales. They were bucketing out a special mix of organic legumes and grains, which the pigs were wolfing down. The Berkshire breed are preferred by many small-scale farmers like Mathers, as the animals have a black skin that can handle the harsh Australian sun. They were originally bred for life outdoors in the English county after which they are named, and are prized for their large frames and marbled flesh. The animals shelter from the sun under established river red gums at the height of the sun and sleep at night in wooden shelters insulated with straw. The pigs do not have their noses pierced. This is a practice used on some outdoor farms in some countries to stop the pigs from turning over the soil. Instead, by the time the herd is moved on, the pasture is turned into a field of dirt, fertilised by the pigs' manure, and ready to be oversown with a pasture crop for the next year.

We stood by a herd of fifty or so pigs grazing on grass then turning the sods with their snouts. I asked Mathers how she could tell if her pigs are happy. 'Well,' she said. 'They do things that look like they are happy. You look at them for a while and you'll see the way they hold their heads and their ears, the arch in their back and the way they interact with each other.' She pointed out random acts of play, when a pig would pick something up and throw it and another pig would take it away, like a game of catch. She explained how she has seen pigs sneaking up on each other, hiding behind one of their shelters and then jumping out to scare another pig. A porky peekaboo. She explained that pigs had different behaviours when they weren't getting along with the rest of the herd, which resemble behaviours of a sick pig. 'They become hunched,' she said. 'They hang their heads. They look depressed. Thankfully, this is extremely rare in our herd.' With that, there is a trill squeal as two young pigs chase each other through the grass, taking turns at who is 'it'.

I have eaten Mathers' pork. It is some of the best in the country. She and her like-minded pig growers have been able to achieve extremely high levels of animal welfare. As Mathers recognises herself, the weak link in this process is the abattoir. By law, all animals slaughtered for sale must go through a licensed abattoir. These are fast-moving and violent places of death for animals and this is something that plays on Mathers' mind.

Back then, Mathers had yet to develop the sangfroid needed to maintain emotional sustainability in a business that saw her send off to slaughter animals she had an emotional connection with. 'I load the pigs onto the trailer and they are wary at first and then it is another adventure to them,' she said. 'And then I hand them over to the abbs (abattoir) and I know what is going to happen to them and what is going to go through their minds and ... and ...' she started to struggle for words. 'And I just start crying. I spend the first twenty minutes driving back home crying. I must have looked a mess.'

LiFE ON THE FARM

I met another pig farmer. One who was constantly criticised for using the term 'bred free range' by the free-range movement. Judy Croagh has Western Plains Pork, a brand known for its quality and consistency. Out in the western volcanic plains past Geelong, she raises 50 000 pigs each year. The sows give birth to their piglets in insulated farrowing huts situated in paddocks. At four weeks the piglets are weaned and raised in eco shelters. These are great domed barns covered with translucent roofs and lined with a deep layer of straw in which the piglets tunnel about and do what piglets do—play. The barns are open to the sky at one end, with a low fence keeping them from escaping.

Croagh stood in the middle of the eco shelter with the pigs for a photograph. The curious young pigs began to mob her like teenagers would Justin Bieber or One Direction. The photo shoot done, she climbed over the barrier. 'When we started out in 1997, we were using the term "bred free range" to try to describe to the market our process,' she said. 'This was happening in a vacuum of regulation and industry oversight.' The fledgling free-range industry were staunch critics, claiming that the term 'bred free range' was a derivative of 'true' free range and was confusing the market. Recently Judy started using the new Australian Pork Industry Quality Assurance Program definition 'outdoor bred'.

This was true. The term 'bred free range' was, through convenience or ignorance, extrapolated to 'free range'. I have witnessed scores of butchers and restaurateurs sell bred-free-range product as free range. At the time of writing, there was a well-known butcher who marketed himself as free range. Like many butchers, he claimed all his meat was free range. 'Just like organic', 'free from … antibiotics' and 'that for no period of time, the animal has been confined to a cage, pen, stall, crate or feedlot.' I have seen where his pork comes from and he is telling pork pies. The pork he sells is outdoor bred. The description of outdoor bred from the Australian Pork Industry Quality Assurance Program reads: 'At weaning piglets move to bedded grow-out housing with adequate feed and water provided where they remain until sale or slaughter. Housing can be permanent or portable structures or outdoor pens with shelter … Pigs may be temporarily confined to pens for routine health treatments and husbandry practices'. This is not 'just like organic'.

The description of outdoor bred and the standards for organic cer-tification differ at many levels. The use of antibiotics would render a pig no longer organic, for example. Outdoor-bred pigs are almost exclusively bred using artificial insemination—something the organic standards do not recommend. I contacted the butcher concerned. He assured me that he no longer stocked outdoor-bred pork and that he now exclusively stocked free-range pork. I said that didn't explain why, as a 'free-range' butcher, he had stocked outdoor-bred pork. His response was a pause, then, 'The problem is that you just can't get enough free-range pork.' That was tacit admission of a lie. He said that in the eyes of the customer there isn't much difference. In reality, it comes down to price. True free range is much more expensive than outdoor bred. That is why there are so many free-range pig farmers selling direct to the customer. If there were a mid-dleman, then the meat would be, in most people's eyes, way too expensive.

The advocates of free-range animal husbandry, however, maintain the difference between the two standards is a matter of chalk and cheese. In so many ways, it is. However, I found myself defending outdoor bred as a way to raise pigs. It is not bad. The pigs were neither agitated nor depressed. They were not chewing each other's tails off. They were not dirty or smelly. There were no burly blokes throwing piglets in the air.

'Pigs don't respond at all well to mistreatment,' Croagh told me. 'If you have people on the team who are attentive and handle the animals properly, then the pigs are more productive,' she explained. 'Stressed pigs, sick pigs, pigs that are forced into unnatural behaviour, they don't do as well. I am a farmer and a businesswoman. We need to maximise the return on our investment in feed, which means making sure there is a high level of animal husbandry.' Croagh has a good number of British and Filipino workers on her farm. She believes they come from cultures where pig farming is respected. 'We are not a nation with a pig-farming culture,' she said. 'Most pigs are raised in intensive feedlots.' She started to describe it as 'the other side of pig farming', then stopped herself. 'I actually can't comment on intensive farming. I have never seen it.'

I have. And I don't like it.

THE FEEDLOT

Several years ago I was writing a story on beef. I was interviewing a senior executive of Certified Australian Angus Beef (CAAB). His company had spent years and invested much in establishing paddock-to-plate traceability of its premium grain-fed beef brand. During the interview he referred to hormone-fed chickens. I knew for a fact that hormones were not used in the Australian chicken industry. Prophylactic antibiotics, yes. As well as a diet that included recycled chicken bits, yes. It was the insistent tone in his voice that alerted me. Knowing he was on the record, was he trying to goad me into propagating a myth about a competitor?

Australian red meat consumption had been falling in favour of white flesh. In 1976 the average Australian ate 66 kilograms of beef and 21 kilograms of lamb each year. By 2011 this had fallen to half: 33 kilograms of beef per person and just 9 kilograms of lamb. Over the same period, the consumption of poultry more than tripled. Similarly, Australians doubled the amount of pork they ate, from 12 kilograms per person in 1976 to 25 kilograms in 2011.

This led me to investigate further. I organised a visit to a feedlot in Central Victoria. This was a cattle feedlot that had supplied cattle to Coles. It was also a feedlot fattening animals for a well-known grower of wagyu. I had read about American feedlots in Michael Pollan's *The Omnivore's Dilemma*. He wrote: 'Animals exquisitely adapted by natural selection to live on grass must be adapted by us … to live on corn, for no other reason than it offers the cheapest calories around'. He writes of appalling conditions where cattle, almost identical to Angus, suffer hideous stomach ulcers, and in which they stand in their own faeces in massive feedlots that create offending sulphurous and ammoniac odours.

What I encountered at that feedlot was quite different. And there is a reason. Much of the food apocalypse literature we read in Australia comes from overseas. We import our food politics. Writers such as Marion Nestle (from the United States), Simon Poole (United Kingdom), Sandor Katz (United States) export quite powerful arguments based on well-researched examples. The only trouble is that the United States and the United Kingdom have quite different food cultures, business models and farming practices to Australia. Milk-inducing hormones are used in the US dairy industry but are not permitted here. While bovine spongiform encephalopathy, or mad cow disease, has infected cattle in the United Kingdom, the United States and Canada, Australia has never had a case. Almost the entire planet is affected with the bee mite varroa that has contributed to, along with systemic pesticides, the dramatic collapse in bee numbers. Bees pollinate 33 per cent of our food crops. At the time of writing, the destructive mite had infected bees as close to Australia as New Zealand. While the Northern Hemisphere, particularly parts of Europe and the United Kingdom, were dusted with the fallout from Chernobyl, Australia was not affected. We don't have a nuclear industry and therefore don't have an underlying unease about atomic accidents. Us reading food-scare lit from the Northern Hemisphere is like Australian kids watching World War II films in the 1970s. These are stories from other countries. And while without drastic food policy changes at every level of government and community we will probably follow the sad path these countries have taken, the stories in imported food-politics literature are not yet our own.

The ICM feedlot outside Wangaratta did not stink. There were no animals standing or lying in faeces. Instead there was a rich smell of fermentation. Some of the feed used, such as corn, is fermented. This emulates the digestive process inside the animal, making the food more nutritious, giving better weight-gain-to-feed ratio. This means the number of kilos eaten by the cow needed to convert to a kilo of muscle or fat. The animals had shade and the floor of the feedlot had ample straw for them to lie down comfortably on. The effluent was collected in ponds and was being treated. It was in no way an ecological or ethical disaster. The animals were well fed and watered.

The general manager, Gina Lincoln, was fresh faced, down to earth and reeked of being a star graduate of an agricultural college. She told me quite openly that part of the feed mix for a good percentage of the animals was made with genetically modified organism (GMO) cottonseed trash. Under Australia's food labelling laws, the meat from an animal fed on GMO fodder does not need to be labelled as such. The rise of GMO crops in Australia will create a supply for GMO-based feeds for the feedlot industry. GMO corn has been approved in Australia.

Lincoln also told me that, depending on the specification of the client, HGP pellets were inserted into the animal's ears. This is hormone growth promotant. It makes cows get heavier faster. Like insecticides and other food chemicals, there is a withholding period. With HGP the last of the hormone is metabolised before the cow is slaughtered. Back then, their client Coles was finishing cattle in the feedlot using HGP to help make them fatter faster. Coles was feeding cattle at the feedlot for around seventy days and trying to get as much weight on as possible. I wrote an article for Fairfax on this topic, following my trip to the feedlot, and after publication, they stopped this practice. At the time of writing, Woolworths, however, continues to use HGP in its beef.

Supermarket cattle being brought into a feedlot to fatten for around seventy days increase their overall weight, but it does little to improve the quality of their flesh. The meat does not 'marble' with fat during this time. The process sees cattle born and raised on farms then trucked to feedlots. These are concrete-lined pens in which a feed mix is delivered to the animals via truck. 'The real change in flavour and marbling happens at the 100 to 150 day mark,' said Lincoln, explaining that marbling describes the fine layers of fat interlacing the muscles. Marbled fat is released into the diner's mouth during chewing, giving a pleasing and juicy sensation. The aroma of the feed, especially corn, gives a nutty flavour to the meat.

But there was something missing. The cows were not—I would not have used the word before, but since I see the word now used freely by the Australian meat industry—happy. The cows were not head-down grazing. Neither were they all on all fours quietly chewing their cud. They were standing. They didn't look like a normal herd. I grew up on a dairy farm and was brought up looking at herds. Animals feed or chew cud, sleep or—well, for want of a herdsman argot—'do cow stuff'. These animals were standing quietly, too quietly. Their heads were a little low, their backs ever so slightly arched. Their tails were ever so slightly lifted. Their back ends were droopy and discharging. This was not all the cows. But to me they looked physically sick and depressed. There is a rule that every hunter, fisher and farmer knows—'You never eat a sick animal'. It was enough to make me never knowingly eat grain-fed beef again.

13

The D Word

She is over it now. But she was treated deplorably. She had argued a good case and presented very well to the packed Melbourne Town Hall. But she mentioned the D word. It proved to be a chink in her armour and ended up overshadowing her and her team's overwhelming success, with a nasty public flaying in which ardent vegans used the post-debate Q and A to attack the vegetarian team.

Veronica Ridge had been asked to take part in an Intelligence Squared debate hosted by the Wheeler Centre and St James Ethics Centre (now called The Ethics Centre) at the Melbourne Town Hall. The topic was 'Animals Should Be Off the Menu'.

Ridge had been asked to take part as former editor of *The Age's Epicure* section, a position she had held for several years. The paper's editor-in-chief, Andrew Jaspan, was a British newspaper man and had previously edited *The Scotsman* in Edinburgh. He wanted to attract new readers to the section by aligning it more to the 'food as politics' sensibilities of the *Observer Food Monthly* in the United Kingdom. 'He wanted less making jam and chocolate cakes on the cover and more Michael Pollan and *Super Size Me*,' said Ridge, referring to the breakout documentary in which a man eats McDonald's every day and accepts the offers of larger fries and Cokes to the detriment of his health, and the works of American food activist Michael Pollan. Ridge was serious about the food section, a lift-out dismissed by a former *Age* editor as the realm of 'soufflé tasters'.

Back when Ridge was appointed editor, the announcement set the foodie world alight. Ridge has been a vegetarian for most of her life. Ed Charles—proto-blogger and an earlier adopter of technology and social media, who quickly realised its capability of disseminating information—took to his website, tomato.com, to publicly decry that a non-meat eater was appointed to the helm of Australia's most respected newspaper food section. There were internal ructions as well, with comments made to management.

Of course it did not pose a problem, and why should it? Ridge promoted a plethora of articles that championed ethical meat and pieces looking at artisanal meat product production. This was good news for me as I suddenly had a lot more work, since I had established my credentials as a writer interested in food production more than food consumption. And that includes meat.

The plan for the debate at Melbourne Town Hall was that Ridge would run whip to intellectual heavyweights ethicist Peter Singer and former Citibank vice-president Philip Wollen (who went on to found the Winsome Constance Kindness trust). The trio had mapped out their game plan well before the debate. Singer was going to argue that meat production was a major polluter and contributor to global warming, saying, 'Livestock production is a bigger contributor to climate change than all transport. Twenty years worth of methane production is seventy-two times more damaging than carbon dioxide.' He also argued that not eating meat was healthier for humans. 'Even small portions of red meat are likely to increase your chance of dying, including from cardiovascular disease, cancer and diabetes,' he argued, citing a study from Harvard University.

Wollen mounted the animal rights argument. In an impassioned speech, he said, 'Animals must be off the menu because tonight they are screaming in terror in slaughterhouses,' describing in detail what he witnessed when he visited abattoirs in his former career as a banker.

'We murder them [animals] at our peril. If slaughterhouses had glass walls, we wouldn't be having this debate tonight.'

Ridge's role was to describe the joys of eating meat-free. In their planning meeting, she brought up the subject of dairy. She was concerned that discussing the ethical raising of cows for milk might lose them the support of the vegans in the audience. She felt that they were needlessly creating an Achilles heel in their argument. Singer and Wollen felt it safest to stick directly to debating the topic 'Animals Should Be Off the Menu'. This meant meat was off the menu. To them, dairy was on the menu but off the table for discussion.

The town hall was packed to capacity, with around 2000 seated in the grand old hall. Audience pre-polling showed that 65 per cent supported the proposition that meat should be off the menu, 22.5 per cent were against, and 12.5 per cent undecided. The atmosphere was rich with a defiant air of anticipation, as if the fans of a reigning football team had landed for an away match in the hometown of a struggling side. It was a social affair with people waving across the packed floor, couples clambering across those already seated to gaps in the rows; the aroma of stale BO, patchouli and self-righteousness hung in the yellow-lit room. The lights lowered and the debate started.

Singer made a compelling case for a meat-free diet being good for human and planetary health. The first speaker for the negative was Fiona Chambers. She is an ethical pig farmer with a small herd who was one of the founders of the rare-breed farm animal movement in Australia. She reasoned that if we don't raise rare-breed livestock for meat then they will become extinct. She then linked soil fertility with livestock grazing, saying that healthy, fertile soils were dependent on rotated grazing and the ensuing manure. This discussion is popular in the ethical farming movement but didn't pass muster in the room stacked with vegetarians. The fumbling of programmes and jiggling of knees suggested the crowd's lack of appreciation for her argument.

Wollen, the former capitalist turned animal activist, was next and debated with the vehemence of a fire-and-brimstone preacher, the rhythm of his delivery evoking call and response. He whipped the audience into a moral froth.

The second speaker for the negative side was animal scientist Bruce McGregor. Acknowledging the impact of Wollen's impassioned performance, he began with a self-deprecating line: 'I'm on a hiding to nothing already,' he said. 'But being a St Kilda supporter, I'm used to it.' This raised a little laugh. He went on to argue that taking animals off the menu would threaten the food security of 'at least two billion people'. The audience were not having any of that, punctuating the air with derisive calls of 'legumes' and 'grain'.

Ridge followed with an eloquent and enthusiastic discourse on the merits of meat-free dining. 'There has been a revolution in vegetarian and vegan cooking and eating in the past decade,' she started. 'A new generation of cooks are using vegetables, pulses, nuts, seeds, herbs and spices in incredible ways. Gone are the mung beans and bland wholemeal pies that accompanied the whiff of 1970s hippiedom.' This dislodged some murmured grumbles from the more curmudgeonly in the crowd. 'In fact,' she continued, 'much of the pleasure and excitement in eating today is this new wave of vegetarian and vegan food that follows an ingredient-led locavore agenda. Let me share a dish with you from Europe's finest vegetarian restaurant, Cafe Paradiso in Cork, Ireland. Its description: feta, pistachio and couscous cakes with sweet and hot pepper jam, citrus greens, coriander yoghurt and spiced chickpeas.'

Days later Ridge trawled through the Twitter feed from the town hall that night. 'As soon as I mentioned "feta" and "coriander yoghurt" the Twittersphere went off,' she says. '"She has lost the argument!!!" declared one Tweeter. The Tweeters were saying that because I was referring to dairy I wasn't in fact taking meat off the menu. There is a link between dairy and veal production.'

The Tweeters in the audience were quick with their censure. The mention of dairy in a vegetarian debate was an act of betrayal. Milk comes from cows. Cows need to calve to make milk. Female calves will most likely join the herd. Male calves are killed at around a week of age. That is the inconvenient truth behind the dairy industry.

Hot on Ridge's heels was Adrian Richardson, a chef known for his love of meat and sausages. He delivered some well-written comic lines with impressive timing. With a more receptive audience, the effort would have been well worth it. Unfortunately, the response was ungenerously flat. 'A few meat-free days and lots of leafy greens will do wonders for the planet and your health,' he said, aligning himself with the affirmative. In a clever piece of strategic argument to win over the room he said, 'If you want to stop factory farming, don't eat supermarket meat. Go to your local butcher: remember him? I'm sure there are some ladies here who do. As long as death is quick and painless, eating animals is okay.' He then declared that the proposition that Animals Should Be Off the Menu was 'ridiculous'. If he had wanted to win the room and not the argument, he couldn't have done much more to offend the crowd, other than biting the head off a chicken.

With the debating part of the night over, the moderator, Simon Longstaff, turned the microphones to the floor of the town hall and had the audience question the debaters. As this was a debate won on the popular vote and not by adjudicators, the battle had not already been lost and won.

Not comfortable with what looked like a win for the vegetarians, the vegans faced up to Ridge, who, as the last speaker, was standing in defence. A clean-shaven and very erudite young man directed a polite but stinging attack on Ridge. He appeared to be on the non-meat eater side, but went for Ridge's jugular. 'Did you know that one of your pin-up chefs is a carnivore?' he asked, throwing the word 'carnivore' down with disdain as if it were synonymous with 'terrorist' or 'paedophile'. 'Did you know that Yotam Ottolenghi eats meat and is a meat eater,' he went on, with a note in his voice that made it sound as if he were clasping both sides of a pulpit in his hands. 'And that Yotam says that he enjoys eating meat?'

Ridge was taken aback. This was an unplanned attack from the flank, coming from what should be considered an ally and unrelated to the point she had made that Ottolenghi's vegetarian recipes created dishes that were easily as innovative and delicious, or more so, than any meat dish. The same person went on to quiz Ridge and her team, asking if any of them had bought a wool suit or leather shoes recently. Wollen, a self-proclaimed changed man from his former wool-suit-and-leather-shoe-wearing, steak-for-corporate-lunch-eating days, stared the young man down by swearing that the only way he could look himself in the mirror was to know that he wore a vinyl belt. This pleased the crowd and they burst into spontaneous applause.

Next to the microphone was an older but just as clean-shaven man, well dressed in country gentleman chic. Chequered blazer, open neck shirt, denim and R.M. Williams boots. 'My name is Michael O'Neill,' he said. 'And I raise ethical cattle.' He went on to describe the high level of ethics he adhered to and the attributes of the animals he raised. He turned to address Ridge directly, but he didn't address her by name. She had published a story about the English White Park rare-breed cattle he and his partner reared on their farm in Central Victoria..

'The third speaker highlighted a number of dishes,' said O'Neill, 'that leading chefs here and internationally all served and held them as a paragon of vegetarianism.' His words were perfectly chosen and carefully delivered. 'Over half of these dishes contain dairy products,' he continued in a very measured but decisive tone. 'One of the principal arguments for the "yes" team is the cruelty aspect and ethics of meat production. Yet the dairy industry is one of the most unethical industries,' he said. 'Dairy products come from milk. For a cow to produce milk the cow has to conceive, and deliver a live birth. What happens in the dairy industry is that progeny is forcefully taken from the mother so the mother can produce obscene amounts of milk. How can they advocate that we eat dishes with dairy products?' Longstaff pulled up the speaker at this point because of time. The room erupted into an anti-dairy outburst of sustained cheers and applause.

This was the attack that Ridge foresaw but was advised not to broach in her prepared debate. Logically 'Animals Should Be Off the Menu' meant that meat, not dairy, was up for debate. The attacks on her argument felt personal. Ridge was a public vegetarian but to those in the room that night had not been vegetarian enough.

Ridge was visibly taken aback and avoided discussing the dairy issue until pressed again by a member of the audience. 'If we had more time I could have offered you a thousand dairy-free dishes,' she said. Longstaff asked her, 'Are you arguing against the dairy industry with the same vehemence as you are arguing against the meat industry?'

Ridge paused. 'Yes,' she answered. 'We are.'

This was a confession extracted under duress. It was a sideshow to the main argument. It was the nasty truth about the dairy industry that was used by both vegans and meat growers. Vegans want all animal products off the menu. Meat producers like to denigrate another industry to confuse and obfuscate the moral argument.

Ridge's team not only won outright, but was able to convince 12.5 per cent of the undecided voters to vote for their cause. They celebrated at a nearby restaurant where animals were definitely off the menu.

THEY SHOOT CALVES, DON'T THEY?

It was dark, cold and still. There was not a star in the moonless sky. A plover cried with its ragged call somewhere further down the hill. You could smell the cows before you heard their heavy breath and snorts. The air was full of the sweet smell of chewed grass and warm breath. Like sniffing the freshest warm milk. It was a familiar scent.

I grew up on a dairy farm and I had never thought of what we did as cruel or unethical. We didn't kill cows. We just milked them. But the anti-dairy sentiment in the Melbourne Town Hall sparked my interest in examining the dairy industry afresh.

I visited two farms. One a modern dairy farm on the Murray River flats west of Echuca. It was large and at its heart it was a motorised rotary dairy servicing 250 cattle twice a day. The cattle were feeding on irrigated pasture and were being supplemented with silage and hay. They were Holsteins: tall, lanky, bony black-and-white animals, all protruding hips and ribs. Just the frame from which to hang a great big udder capable of producing nearly 50 litres of milk each day.

Dairy cattle are bred to produce calves efficiently and safely. Without a calf, cows do not lactate. Dairy cattle are also bred to produce large quantities of protein-rich milk. Smaller Jersey and Guernsey cows produce less milk but it is much higher in butterfat. Milk protein and butterfat are exportable commodities derived from cow's milk. Echuca is a dry area and it seemed ironic that farmers spend a fortune irrigating their crops with water while the processors spend a fortune on electricity to separate and dehydrate the milk.

Milk herd cattle are generally artificially inseminated. Pregnant cattle are removed from the herd and placed with other pregnant mothers. At birth, calves spend the first twelve hours to a few days with their mother to drink the all-important, but commercially unsuitable, colostrum. This is the nutrient- and enzyme-rich secretion that is produced by a mammal's mammary glands after birth. It has a different nutrient composition from the milk that follows. After this, the calves are separated from their mothers.

To separate calves and mothers is distressing for all concerned. The mother and calf bellow for each other for days afterwards. To say that a cow can make a mournful sound is an understatement. When you take her calf away a cow searches for her infant in an imploring voice that has evolved to penetrate forests and pass through valleys. Some mothers will break through fences to get back with their calves. Bonding and motherhood are instincts that breeders can't eliminate from dairy cattle. Once separated, the mothers are returned to the milking herd, where they are milked twice a day. Our family milked cows during the 1950s to 1980s. We had a small herd of just forty cows. They would be milked for nine to ten months, around 300 days, then were dried off. Most of the 'girls', as they were referred to, stayed with us until they were around ten years old. Now the average Australian dairy cow is milked for 400 days and slaughtered when she is three to four years old. In large dairy areas there are specialist 'chopper cow' abattoirs specialising in ex-dairy cows. Here cows are slaughtered, and flesh stripped from the bone, boxed, frozen and shipped to the United States, where they will become hamburger mince.

While some breeders have been able to breed cattle without horns, or 'polled', most cattle are born with their horns intact. Both male and female cattle have horns. The reason you don't see dairy cows with horns is because they have their horns removed. A cow with horns won't fit into the bale when she is being milked. The bale is the trough from which she eats energy-rich food when she is being milked. This is part of the feed regime and part bribe. The horns can be burned off while they are at bud stage. This is when the bone and skin is removed either with a red-hot iron or with a chemical. Fully-grown horns can be removed later with a guillotine-like dehorner that cuts through the live bone. I have seen both processes and it is clearly painful. They bellow, snort, froth at the mouth and their eyes roll around in their heads.

Almost all male calves and three-quarters of the female calves don't have to worry about getting dehorned. These are the 'bobby' calves. It's a cute name. These are the calves that are surplus to requirement. Only about a quarter of each season's calves are required to replace their mothers in the milking herd. The rest become bobby calves. In almost all cases, male calves are consigned to bobby-calf status, as artificial insemination is the industry norm. Bobby calves are held on the farm for a minimum of five days. During this period they can be fed the colostrum or powdered milk replacement. After this they can legally be shipped to market. Some of the calves will be raised to become veal or rose veal, adding a few more months to their life. (Some of the young females will find themselves on a plane or boat to establish herds in China.) The rest are slaughtered as young calves. Their pelts are made into leather goods, their bones ground for fertiliser, their tissues harvested for the pharmaceutical industry. The trip to the abattoir for a calf can be a long one. At this stage of life they haven't learned herd behaviours, so rounding up calves is metaphorically similar to rounding up cats. It's frustrating for all concerned. And stressful for the calves. The bobby calves are penned overnight and not given a drink before the next morning. Tired, stressed, thirsty and hungry the next morning, the bobby claves are given a bolt gun to the head, then everything turns to black.

Although much larger than the farm I grew up on, it was a pretty similar operation and work practices had not changed much in the last forty years. The narrative our family and our community of dairy farmers had developed to describe what we did for a living was a gentle lie. It was a cover story, a false narrative, to blur and obfuscate the reality of the misery we were causing in the name of earning a living. We even invented a pretty and inoffensive little word: 'bobby'. It's easier to live with than 'killing baby calves'.

I love dairy. I like drinking milk (unhomogenised, at the very least) and I enjoy cheese. I will forgo dessert in a restaurant for a white mould, washed rind and blue cheese. Which is why I was trudging around this other dairy farm, in the green hills of Gippsland's Strzelecki Ranges, one pitch-black winter's morning.

Walking next to me was a dairy farmer with a different way of raising her herd and a different business model. Vicki Jones is a quietly spoken woman. I could barely make out her outline in the dark but she seemed petite for someone who spends her life with such large and heavy animals. Her voice has a lovely high yet mellifluous quality. If she sang, I imagine she would sound like Minnie Riperton.

On Jones's farm, Mountain View Organic Dairy, south of Warragul in West Gippsland, a completely new model of dairy farming has been created, not from a period of researching and reflecting on existing food-political business practices, but from an existential crisis. To her it was a spiritual dilemma.

'Killing calves? It's like killing children,' she said quietly. 'It's psychotic.' Jones walked quietly through the barely visible herd. They were lying down in the shelter of a row of pine trees and you could hear them breathe and their teeth grind through wads of cud. They lazily got up. Backs legs first. Front legs kneeling. Front legs straightening. These cows were not as big as the ones on the other farm near Echuca. They were smaller, fatter and somehow more amiable. 'To have an industry that creates live animals as a waste stream is ridiculous,' she says as she slowly wakes her herd. 'It is insane.'

With a glow welling on the eastern horizon, silhouettes of the cows could be made out against the pre-dawn sky. Between the legs of some of the cows appeared another finer set of legs. Calves. Jones does not systematically remove calves from their mothers. Some she lets stay to be raised by their mothers.

In a normal economic dairy model, calves are a liability. They consume the product one is making with little return. It would be like a lettuce grower keeping caterpillars or a forester burning a quarter of his wood. Running a dairy farm is a costly business. The power bill to run the machinery and to bring thousands of litres of milk down from the body temperature of 38 degrees Celsius to a safe temperature of under 4 degrees Celsius costs Jones $4000 a quarter. In larger dairies you can triple this figure. On top of this there are feed, veterinary medicine, fencing, fertiliser, labour, diesel and other costs and outgoings. At the time of writing, the average farmgate price for a litre of milk was 50 cents. Farmgate price is the gross price the processor gives the farmer. From this, he or she has to pay wages, electricity, gas, rates and bank loan interest, and buy feed, cleaning chemicals, farm machinery, fertiliser, fencing wire and other sundry items before they bank whatever, if any, is left over. 'A dairy farming friend of ours is losing $100000 for every million litres of milk he produces,' said Jones as we head towards the dairy, a blob of green fluorescent light on the hill ahead. 'The only reason why we have a dairy industry in Australia is that families are borrowing money against their farms and working incredibly long hours with little return.' She paused. 'It is a form of indentured labour. The dairy industry in Australia is broken and in its present form is not sustainable.'

In 2007, in the midst of the millennial drought, Jones found herself bleeding money. The price of fuel had gone up and despite her living in one of the most fertile places with some of the best rainfall in Australia, she had to buy in food for her animals. She was angry and wanted change.

She contacted the CEO of Dairy Australia, asking that a concerted effort be made to raise the price of milk. He responded, 'You think it fair that people should pay more for their milk?' Jones was flabbergasted. "If people want dairy farmers to be around in the future," I thought, "Of course it is fair people pay more for their milk".' Jones's soft voice trembled a little.

She and her husband worked out a different model of how to make a living from a dairy herd. They realised that the bobby calves are actually an asset. They could be raised for beef. Older cows in their herd and cows that presented with ongoing mastitis (an udder condition that renders their milk unsuitable for further processing) were sent to other pastures to raise the bobby calves. Those mothers whose maternal instincts were very well developed were allowed to keep their calves until they were weaned. 'Instead of seeing animals as either being productive or nonproductive we saw value in every animal in every stage of its life,' said Jones. 'It's about empathy. I am not a person who can commit an animal to a life of misery,' she said matter-of-factly.

Jones doesn't remove her animals' horns. For her it is simply too cruel. She is slowly breeding horns out of her herd by crossing her cows with a bull, using a breed called Aussie Reds, itself a mix of Scandinavian old-fashioned milk breeds and modern genetics. For Jones, her milk production is not about volume but quality and taste. She does not sell her milk to a large factory or dairy cooperative. Instead she has a client base of around 300 families to whom she sells dairy products and meat. Her customers want milk that is full flavoured with plenty of fat. Fat in milk in a carton has been standardised to 3.8 per cent. Milk comes out of most good cows, depending on the season, at 4 per cent. Jones's milk is 5 per cent butterfat.

Dairy cows are not known for their flesh. While meat-breed cows produce quite white fat, dairy cows tend to produce yellow to deep yellow fat, something modern meat eaters have been steered away from by the meat-industry marketing people. The flesh from dairy cows can also be considerably more flavoursome. Jones has been able to educate her customers that yellow fat is good and that the full flavour is desirable. Her animal husbandry is of a very high standard. Her cows spend eleven productive years in the herd before being moved off into the nursery herd. Their 'cell count', or 'plate count', is low. This refers to the number of different organisms and quantity thereof that is found in the milk. The lower the plate count the healthier the milk. It's an indication of not only the health of the udder but of the cow herself.

We were almost at the dairy. There the ground was soft and the mud deep and sticky. Deep and sticky enough to pull your gumboots off. Jones explained that she grows her bobby calves out to adulthood. The females rejoin the milking herd, and the young males are castrated and allowed to grow for fifteen to twenty-four months before being slaughtered.

We were outside the dairy now and the pale light spilled out into the dark, lighting up Jones's face. She has delicate features and quizzical eyes, framed by brown hair topped with a beanie. I asked her what is the difference between killing an animal when it is an infant or killing it when it is an adult. Jones's gentle demeanour became harder. She squared up. 'Richard,' she said. 'You are going to die. Agree? Well, why don't I kill you right now? It makes no difference,' she argued rhetorically. 'I want farmers to have the opportunity to raise calves for beef and not have to kill them. I want there to be another way.' Inside the dairy there was a smaller rotary dairy set up. The cows walked themselves into the yards and into the dairy. They were bright, alert, with a good covering of flesh on their frames. Jones's husband placed the milking cups on the cows' teats and looked up at his wife and smiled. Jones reciprocated and looked at her herd with a broad grin. 'I don't think it is acceptable that dairy farmers are enmeshed in this cycle of death. Animals want to live. It is pretty obvious.'

All Vicki Jones's words rang true in April 2016 when the two large dairy processors in Australia, Murray Goulburn and New Zealand-owned Fonterra, cut milk prices overnight and demanded farmers repay the money the processors had paid to them. It was a hellish scene in the country with stories of farmer suicides dominating over-the-gate conversations while in the city the public turned their ire towards the supermarkets, leaving Coles and Woolworths' $1 milk to curdle on the shelves in favour of more costly, branded milk. The truth of the matter was that milk was no longer profitable. Every litre customers purchased was still sending farmers deeper into debt as the cost of production was 1 cent a litre higher than the farm-gate price.

14

Reasons to Celebrate

When I was five I planted my first vegetable garden. It was in a strip of earth that ran parallel to the weatherboards outside my brothers' bedroom. It was autumn and the earth was cold and wet. I remember pulling out some weeds and collecting some manure from under the cypress trees to dig into the soil. My father must have turned the soil for me, as the earth was loose and pliable when I planted the seeds. The seeds were hard, large and round and had what looked like a bottom on one end. I had been given them to plant by a grown-up and I did not know what they were going to grow into. They also had what looked like one eye winking out of the other end. They were rude and amusing but could also see. I had watched my father plant seeds in straight lines, poking them deep into the earth with his fingers, a good distance apart. So I did the same.

I went out every morning after I planted the seeds to see if they had grown. Never underestimate the sense of joy and achievement in a child when the seed they have planted emerges from the earth. The dual-leafed seedlings looked like rows of little men with bowed heads, the shell of the seed sitting on top like monks' hoods. The seedlings grew over winter and by the time it was September holidays they were towering stalks. Bean stalks. Broad-bean stalks studded with white and black flowers. They were so high. I could stand among them and I could see the sky and clouds through their sharp-ended leaves. The aroma was sweet and delicious. The buds withered and little bean pods emerged. They were soft and spongy, and if you looked closely were covered in fine white hair. When very small, broad beans are very sweet. As they grow they have more texture and get more flavoursome, but that sweetness turns to bitterness.

That spring was my first season of broad beans. I was eager to pick them but was told to wait. 'Wait until they are bigger and then there will be more for everyone.' I waited for a few hours. We had them steamed with lamb chops. We ate lamb chops or steak with all our vegetables. The broad beans were small, fresh, sweet and, most importantly, I had grown and picked them myself.

At the end of winter they are the vegetable that I most crave. Spring is not a time of bounty. It is actually one of the leanest harvest times of the year. The winter veg are finishing and most summer fruit and vegetables' are just starting their journey from bloom to ripening. But there are a handful of vegetables that mark the start of the year. Along with broad beans, peas, asparagus and artichokes mark the start of spring.

During a recent spring I was working on a baking book with Melbourne baker Phillippa Grogan. During the process of the book, called *Phillippa's Home Baking*, she led me through a steep learning curve in baking while I showed her the path to book writing. I had never made good bread before I worked on that book. Sure, I had followed the recipe on the side of a packet of Tandaco Dry Yeast, but always ended up with a scone-like texture that tasted like unfermented yeast. As I found out, a lot of bread recipes call for lots of yeast to make the dough rise quickly. Phillippa taught me to use less yeast and let the dough ferment for a longer period. The yeast was allowed to multiply in its own time. The result was bread with a more complex flavour, a crisper crust and a more even and better crumb. By the end of the winter I was baking every day to perfect the process and understand the technique. Which is when I discovered breadcrumbs.

With so much bread lying around and not enough gluten-tolerant neighbours to give it away to, I had to find a way of dealing with the excess. I turned the bread into breadcrumbs. Breadcrumbs blended with rosemary, thyme, parmesan and garlic. The Moulinex blender got a real workout. This mix that makes a perfect coating for eggplant parmigiana. It works just as well on zucchini, broccoli and cauliflower. It perfects cauliflower cheese and, when fried, tops off steamed broccoli brilliantly, particularly when it is folded through al dente orecchiette and finished with a little more parmesan and a little extra virgin olive oil. Breadcrumbs went onto the top of everything that season.

One dish that I learned from Melbourne chef Ian Curley, from The European, is pasta primavera. (Ironic, but typical of Melbourne, that I live in one of the largest Italian diaspora cities in the world and get taught an Italian classic by a Pom.) It's a springtime staple at his bistro opposite Parliament House. It is also a very, very simple dish of broad beans, peas, asparagus, parmesan, fried breadcrumbs and extra virgin olive oil served with some pasta. You can cut out the pasta, and make the breadcrumbs much larger by tearing apart old bread into very small pieces—the Spanish call these *migas* (diminutive of *hormigas*, or ants)—and fry them in lots of olive oil. *Migas* are also excellent with steamed broad beans.

That spring I realised just how well broad beans go with new potatoes and mint. By letting the warm salad sit together, the potatoes release some starch into the dressing and absorb some of it, in turn creating a rich and satisfying dish.

Just as rich and satisfying is the way that fresh broad beans, cooked in loads of butter, garlic and breadcrumbs, make a very pleasing dip. It works as well on crudités as it does with grissini, and is particularly nice with a buttery Australian chardonnay.

Another spectacularly simple dish I worked on is based on the technique from Raymond Capaldi's pumpkin soup recipe. This involves, however, asparagus that is gently sautéd in butter until just soft, seasoned, then pureed with stock in a high-speed blender and served with goat's cheese and extra virgin olive oil.

By that spring I had not been eating meat for more than six months. I no longer craved that golden brown, slightly salty crusted roast/chicken thigh/steak/roast pork, or insert any other description of cooked meat. I found that I was more aware of different sorts of hunger. Sometimes I felt like I needed starch. So I would cook a bowl of brown rice and add some curry sauce. Sometimes I really felt like I needed green. Powerful, strong green. Silverbeet. Rocket. Spinach. Other times I would spend a day in the country photographing the characters and iconic buildings and attractions of a town for a column I had been working on every week for several years, and really need to chow down on a lentil burger. Not the bun, but the yellow split peas that make up the patty. Sometimes it was the green tang and European aroma of dill I wanted to consume. Loads of dill. Chopped dill mixed with mint. Chopped dill mixed with mint, rolled through sour cream and fondled through handfuls of leaves. Chicory. Mizuna. Rocket. Lettuce.

Then there was a dish I often craved. Had done for decades and still do. It's saag paneer, a classic dish from North India. Spinach and spices are cooked to a creamy consistency with the zing of ginger and turmeric. Pieces of firm cheese are added to the mixture. It is a really bright and spicy sauce that enriches rice. It is nutrient dense and not very much makes you feel quite full.

That spring I returned to see my mate chef Rosa Mitchell. Her little Italian restaurant on the edge of Chinatown in Melbourne was kicking along. She was born Rosa Pagano in Sicily sixty years ago. She moved to Australia when she was a very young girl, so speaks English like an Aussie and Italian like a Sicilian peasant. What she lacks in height she makes up for in sheer exuberance for life. Her mains menu, at the beginning of this particular spring, was thick with meaty dishes like spatchcock with rosemary, vino cotto and potato. Snapper with stewed broad beans, cauliflower and mint. Rabbit cooked in marsala with rosemary on a bed of pearl barley. Slow-cooked pork with borlotti beans and fennel. Tongue, potatoes and *salmoriglio*—a fresh sauce made with olive oil, lemon, garlic, parsley and oregano. In true peasant form, all of Rosa's dishes were based on a tradition where the meat is used as a condiment for the starch and vegetables. It was possible to remove the flesh from every one of those dishes and still end up with a delicious meal.

Instead, I opted for the *contorni*. This is a little secret I learned during the My Year Without Meat project. Go for the sides. Go for '*contorni*'. You can order a meat-free meal with plenty of nutrition by going for the sides. The sides are where you'll find good seasonal vegetables and salads that taste good and will sustain you, without having to eat your body weight in the processed starch of pasta or white rice risotto. On the sides menu this day was a plate of broccolini with garlic, pecorino and fried breadcrumbs. Then there was a dish of artichokes, small pieces of potato baked in a little stock and lemon juice, and lots of parsley. Perhaps the most stunning dish was a plate of sweet and sour pumpkin cooked with whole quills of cassia. It could have been a dish from Morocco. It could have been Indian. They were are all stunning and they made me feel good. 'That is the beauty of the simple peasant foods,' said Rosa. 'They are really adaptable. We can have a table of vegos, gluten free and dairy free and feed the lot with basically the same menu with very little stress on the kitchen. That's the beauty of cooking traditional dishes.'

With a finer-tuned palate I began to seek out better-quality fruit and veg with missionary-like zeal. I found that by buying at a mix of farmers' markets, markets and supermarkets the quality of the produce seemed to follow. The fruit and veg from farmers' markets lasts longer than that from the market and much longer than that from the supermarket. The flavour tends to be stronger and the texture firmer.

It was that spring that my understanding of the true beauty of great fruit and vegetables was really awakened. There is a depth of character in really ripe, ready and fresh produce. In great beetroot there is an aroma that is like raspberries or cherries mixed with chocolate. Fresh rocket has a pleasant bitterness that matches the bright zing of its chlorophyll. The best lettuce is slightly 'to the tooth', with a sharp tang from the white milk running through the ribs. (Lettuce's botanical name is *Lactuca sativa*. The genus name comes from the Latin *lact*, because of the milky nature of the sap. Lettuces were originally a medicinal food and the sap was much more bitter. That bitterness has been bred out of lettuce over the centuries, so lettuces now have almost no taste.)

One brisk Saturday morning I visited a farmers' market, scanning the crowd for friends and colleagues, but the early spring chill had kept most of them in bed. I went to my mate Michael Zandegu. He was the chef who had asked me six months earlier if there was something wrong with me because I had given up meat. Back then he was cooking next to a butcher at farmers' markets. Now he was on his own, away from the butcher, and serving breakfasts that involved lots of fermented vegetables, polenta, poached eggs, popped grains and kale. He looked like a younger version of Al Delvecchio from *Happy Days*. 'Here,' he said. 'Try this,' proffering a purple frond of a leaf. 'It's red mizuna from a customer's backyard. Eat it.' It was delicious. Crisp, hot, peppery, a clean finish with layers of flavour. There was rocket as well. The fine-leafed baby rocket. 'It's good, isn't it?' he said. 'You know what you do with really good rocket?' he asked rhetorically. 'Nothing. Good rocket needs nothing. You know why people put Parmigiano on rocket? Because it is gutless, tasteless shit that is more or less grown hydroponically. It has never seen soil, so has no flavour or nutrition. The same with lettuce,' he continued. 'Iceberg lettuce from a supermarket? It is just filler. Filler for American hamburgers. The Americans cut the lettuce so it sits as a bed to offer textural contrast but no flavour. Modern lettuce *has* no flavour and *no* goodness. Modern vegetables grown under modern conditions are tasteless and more or less useless.' He offered another green from his friend's garden. It was green mizuna. It was even more peppery and tasty and filled my mouth with a lasting zing.

Earlier that year, before I had given up meat, I wanted to explore the basics of biodynamic agriculture. I had driven to Powelltown, a small settlement in the forest of the Great Dividing Range separating the Yarra Valley from Gippsland. This is the headquarters of Alex Podolinsky, the man considered by many to be the father of biodynamics in Australia. (The biodynamic movement in Australia is divided into two chapters. Podolinsky runs the more dogmatic of the two). Erudite and energetic, he spoke with a gentle Russian accent, emitting a Yoda-like wisdom that must be fathomed by understanding his riddles and quests. Podolinsky doesn't preach. He either turns people away or sets them on a path of learning.

Podolinsky walked me towards his shed. The garden was surrounded by forest with lush paddocks, and there was a small warehouse where the Biodynamic Marketing Company distributes food to retailers. The Podolinsky family were fundamental in establishing biodynamics in Australia. Inside the small shed were sacks filled with cow horns stacked to the rafters. To the detractors of the biodynamic movement, cow horns are both the lightning rod that attacks criticism and the proof that it is at best pseudoscience and at worst witchcraft. Detractors make comments that horns are filled with magic potion.

Podolinsky explained that it wasn't magic potion in the cows' horns but manure. Each horn had been filled with fresh cow manure months earlier and buried in the earth over winter. Over the winter the manure had changed and matured into a substance that the biodynamic community refers to as Preparation 500.

Podolinsky held a small plug of the 500 in the palm of his hand and spelled out the differences between organics and biodynamics. 'While organic certification requires the exclusion of chemicals, biodynamics is about the creative input,' he said. 'Creating humus to hold soil nutrients. My aim is to make our farmers observe what is happening on their farm and think biologically. I see our farmers as creative composers.' He explained that founder Rudolf Steiner identified nine different 'preparations' numbered from 500 to 508 that were fundamental to plant health. He explained that the word biodynamic comes from the Ancient Greek *bios*, meaning life, and *dynamis*, meaning power or energy. It was coined after Steiner's death.

Podolinsky spread the Preparation 500 out in his hands. The material that at the beginning of winter was wet, green and shitty was now putty-like and neutral smelling. In it were billions of microbes and particles of trace elements that would be stirred through water and sprayed over a farm, garden or vineyard.

To the uninitiated, Podolinsky's words seemed confusing. To me it seemed that he was not there to initiate me into his sect, but was acting as a gatekeeper barring my entrance. The terminology used by the biodynamic movement is a jargon that does little to describe the simple but quite remarkable transformations that take place in the soil and in plants when Mother Nature is allowed to go about her own work without the interference of man-made compounds and techniques.

It was suggested by one of Podolinsky's employees that I have a conversation with a biodynamic farmer. It was late summer and the sun was beating down on his orchard on the banks of the Leigh River at Inverleigh. This is an old staging post between Geelong on Port Phillip Bay and Hamilton, some 200 kilometres to the west. It is a very pretty little town, made up of bluestone buildings and modern houses perched above the Leigh River, which flows through a gorge lined with river red gums.

Darren Aitken was fit and wiry, with an open face and broad grin. He led us to the orchard; long grass was growing knee high, little bugs and grasshoppers flying up as we disturbed them. A flock of chickens chased the bugs in the lazy warmth. A few ducks were nibbling on the lowest-hanging and ripest of the fruit hanging from boughs.

I had been warned that I would come back converted. 'It's a cult,' said one farmer I know. 'It's full of nutters who believe in cosmic energy and magic potions stored in cow horns,' said the owner of a local independent wine store. Their assumptions were based on a core of information that was ostensibly correct, it was just that the assumptions had altered the veracity. The biodynamic movement is based on the teachings of early twentieth-century Austrian philosopher Steiner. He was a man who combined the teachings of science and spiritualism to create a movement he described as anthroposophy. His teachings were adopted and coopted by organisations as benign and wholesome as the Steiner kindergartens we see today, as well as those with slightly more malevolent intent, such as Germany's National Socialists, also known as Nazis. Because he combined science, which can be proved, with spiritualism, which can only be believed, he has been reviled.

I asked Aitken about his use of cosmic energy. He took a well-weathered hand and raised it to the sun. 'That,' he said, using carefully chosen words, 'is cosmic energy. Energy from the cosmos beaming direct to us here on Earth.' He broke into a smile. 'It's sunlight. Plants use it to photosynthesise,' he said matter-of-factly. 'I use it to grow my produce. Just as every farmer does.' Aitken paused to let the information sink in. 'I know the term "cosmic energy" puts some people off but that's what sunlight is. Plants capture it. We dig the plants into the soil. The soil becomes more fertile.'

What he was describing is the form of agriculture that was prevalent across the globe prior to World War II. At its heart is photosynthesis. This is a silent and unstoppable process that occurs wherever there are plants, air, water and sunlight. Plants take carbon dioxide from the air and water through their roots and, using photons from the sun, break apart the carbon dioxide and water molecules, in cells called chloroplasts, reformulating them into carbohydrate and oxygen. Carbohydrate in the form of simple sugar, monosaccharide in the form of glucose and in different forms of starch or polysaccharides from pectin to lignin. It happens all around us, in our house plants, the potatoes in our veggie patch, the weeds in the footpath. To me it is a miracle.

As we walked through his orchard, Aitken continued to explain that the energy of the sun, now captured in new plant growth, is then ploughed back into the earth. The grass growing between the apple trees in his orchard would be mown down and ploughed back into the soil or covered with more mulch. Microbes in the soil would then break the grass down into humus. They would break down the manure from the chickens and ducks into humus as well. Humus is a spongy material made of plant matter, the faeces of worms, insects and microbes themselves. It is packed with energy and nutrients, and holds lots of water.

'One of the ideas of biodynamics is that you don't need to bring extra inputs onto the farm,' Aitken explained. 'It's a closed system. You use what occurs naturally to create more life.' This also includes creating great piles of compost made from hay, manures and the stalks and stems from plants that are surplus after harvest. Aitken bent down and tore out a lump of dark earth that looked like rich chocolate cake, except for the teeming numbers of worms and insects. 'It's the life you can't see that really matters,' said Aitken. He squeezed a handful of soil and it stuck together like moist black breadcrumbs. 'This is colloidal humus. It can hold 75 per cent of its own weight in water.'

Running just under the surface of the lump of soil was what appeared to be a dense and random spider's web. This was explained to me as being mycorrhizal fungi. 'What we think of as being fungus are mushrooms and toadstools,' explained Aitken. 'But these are just the fruiting body of the fungus'. Mycorrhizal fungus itself is a network of threads that interlace the soil and that can spread over many square metres, and can, in some circumstances, cover entire hectares of land, particularly in forests.

I had seen mycorrhizal fungi growing earlier in the year, when I was walking with a mushroom expert, Alison Pouliot. We were in a clearing in a forest in Central Victoria and she pointed out a 'fairy ring' of mushrooms. Common *Agaricus bisporus* or field mushrooms. The mushrooms were in a rough circle about the size of a small car. Some of the mushrooms were older than others and some were just emerging from the grass in the clearing. Two things were noticeable: the ring itself, and the darker colour of the grass within and just around the ring.

I hadn't understood why the grass was a darker colour until Aitken explained more about the relationship between the plants and the fungus. What goes on underground is a complex and symbiotic system of barter and exchange between the fungus and the flowering plants on the surface. The plants provide the fungus with glucose, and the fungus provide the plants with essential and trace elements. The fungus's very fine threads interlock with the roots of the plants in a consenting and penetrative embrace. The plant's roots have special receptacles that have evolved to accept the delivery of nutrients from the fungus and the passing of energy to the fungus in the form of simple sugar. By doing this the plant can extend its effective root cover to hundreds of square metres. This symbiotic relationship is in no way specific to biodynamic farming; however, the very practices biodynamic farmers embrace proliferate this silent and cheap army working underground to create healthier plants.

Sometimes the relationship between plant and fungus is specific. Autumn foragers heading to the countryside in search of pine mushrooms will be well aware that in order to find the mushrooms, they need to head to the pine forests and pine trees growing in considerable numbers. Under them they look for circles of *Lactarius deliciosus*, the salmon-coloured mushroom much sought after by old Italian couples, *en trende* chefs and hipster foodies. Pine trees and pine mushrooms have one of these special relationships. In the early days of the pine plantations, Australian foresters were puzzled as to why they couldn't get their Monterey pines, or *Pinus radiata*, to grow as high and prolifically as they did in their native Californian coastal habitat. The growing conditions in southern Australia were similar enough to achieve success but the early seedlings in the plantations would take, then fail to thrive. It wasn't until foresters visited similar pine plantations in New Zealand that they noticed the pine trees of a similar age there were green, robust and doing very well. The difference was that the New Zealand foresters were inoculating the roots of their seedlings with a solution that contained the spores of *Lactarius deliciosus*. With the fungus working silently underground foraging for nutrients, the pine trees were able to grow to their full potential. New Zealanders are true to their canny Scottish roots, and the foresters there established a complementary income to that from their trees by harvesting and selling the mushrooms, giving them an income stream long before the pines were ready to be chopped down for timber.

Aitken explained that the formulation of his preparations was time consuming, that the creation and turning of compost was laborious, and the mulching of the soil was backbreaking. Aitken, however, does not spray pesticides or apply fertiliser, in itself not only time consuming but also very expensive, with the cost of the chemicals compounded by the cost of fuel and labour. The more machinery drives over the earth, the more compacted it becomes, which can disrupt the network of fungi. The effects of fertilisers and chemicals on mycorrhizal fungi are not clearly understood across a broad range of the horticultural community. It has been explained to me that if a plant has its basic nutritional needs met by artificially formulated nitrogen, phosphorus and potassium fertiliser (N, P and K), then those bonds formed with the fungus underground are diminished and other complementary elements are no longer forthcoming.

Aitken explained that because of the way he grows his vegetables, they are healthier. Because they are healthier they are able to resist pest attack. Having given up his chemical armoury, Aitken, like other biodynamic growers, relies on other forms of pest control and avoidance. He breaks up his crops so they don't appear as a monoculture to attacking insects. Some biodynamic farmers opt for 'peppering' in which the pest weed, for example, is burned and its ashes spread about. Others use more practical solutions. One biodynamic orchardist I heard about had a problem with codling moth, a bug that lives under the old bark. His solution? He hired a sandblaster and removed the old bark. Problem solved.

I took away more with me that day than new understanding. I was laden with a box of Aitken's produce. It was some of the best food I have ever seen. Aromatic, beautifully shaped, green leafed and firm stalked. The five different varieties of rhubarb were sweet and pleasantly earthy, with some carrying the faint fragrance of tea roses. The unifying experience of tasting his produce was a sensation of feeling sated. I understood that it wasn't just vegetables that I was craving, but good vegetables. Like the difference between the cheap ethanol fuel one puts into the hire car on the way back to the airport and the high-octane stuff you pump into your car to buzz around town. Both are called unleaded but the differences in the running of your car are very apparent. Same with veg. Some just don't have the taste, the flavour and that ability to make you feel good.

THE BLOW OUT

I am a food writer. I drink. It is part of the job description. Sometimes I drink too much. That is not part of the job description. What follows I am not proud of. That spring I was preparing for a mate's birthday party. His present was a paella and slow-cooked leg of lamb, to be shredded and served in bread rolls with gravy and mint sauce the following evening. Although not eating meat myself, I was not emphatic that others should not also, so I had no problem in cooking the meal.

Prepping paella for sixty people involves lots of chopping. One has to chop up loads of red capsicum and tomato to make the *sofrito*. You could do this in a blender but the blades do too much damage at a cellular level. This releases too much water, which means that the *sofrito* effectively boils at 100 degrees Celsius. This in turn stops the caramelisation of the sugars and slows the Maillard reaction, which adds to its colour and flavour. Anyway—it's best to chop the ingredients for a paella by hand. It is a repetitive chore that requires speed to get through the two sinks filled with vegetables. One with tomatoes and the other with red capsicums. Speed and skill. Skill with a knife is essential. Chopping at speed requires concentration. And what better way to concentrate than drinking pinot noir. And after the first bottle and one sink full of vegetables, perhaps another bottle.

Meanwhile, in the oven had gone two whole shoulders of lamb. They were complete with neck and leg, giving them a slightly sinister Snowtown quality. (A reference to the small South Australian town perched somewhere between arable land and the outback, where police made the grizzly find of eight bodies decomposing in barrels. There is a butcher there who sells perhaps the best saltbush mutton in Australia. Years ago, on a trip back from a filming expedition, I stopped there and bought our small crew gifts of legs of mutton to take home.)

The lamb shoulders were laid out on big trays, and sitting on a bed of hard-leafed herbs from the garden: bay, rosemary and thyme. I had preheated the oven to 260 degrees Celsius. The shoulders had been covered in olive oil and rubbed with salt. After a good thirty to forty minutes the skin had browned and crisped. I reduced the heat to around 100 degrees and allowed the shoulders to cook slowly while I chopped away, quietly slugging pinot noir and listening to BBC programmes on ABC NewsRadio. Somewhere between National Public Radio Morning Edition and the end of the second bottle of pinot noir, the capsicums and tomatoes were finally all chopped, incident free, and sealed in great plastic boxes in the fridge, and the golden lamb shoulders removed from the oven. The kitchen was redolent of garden herbs and sweet, soft lamby flesh. I sat on the couch to wait for them to cool, the last of the pinot splashed in the glass in my hand, and Leonard Cohen's 'Tower of Song' now playing very loudly on the stereo.

I woke up the next morning with a heaviness in my stomach, to find the kitchen cleaned, as I had left it, and the legs of lamb in the fridge. I must have wrapped them up and put them away before I went to bed. There was one small issue. One of the legs was missing several sizeable chunks of flesh. The entire calf muscle on the shank and the muscle that sits next to the scapula on the shoulder itself. The meat was wrapped, if not particularly well, in cling film, and the dog was still locked in the laundry. No one else was awake in the house, and whole muscles of meat are not things small female children are likely to squirrel back to their rooms for an impromptu midnight feast. There was a greasiness around my mouth and a familiar lanolic tang. There was a sensation in my back molars I had not experienced in some months. Short strings of muscle. Lamb muscle.

I had, in my stupor, eaten a fair portion of one of the shoulders of lamb. Hangover notwithstanding, I felt terrible; for I had almost half a kilogram of lamb sitting in my stomach that I was having trouble digesting.

I was in an ethical dilemma. Would this put an end to My Year Without Meat? What would I say to my editors? Would people smell meat on my breath? Luckily I had been a keen student of the Renaissance and Reformation and was keenly aware of the old Catholic custom of indulgences. An indulgence was a ticket of leave, as it were, for a wealthy person to commit carnal, mortal and deadly sins. By paying a hefty tax to Rome, they could have people pray on their behalf and save their soul from hell or, even worse for some, its slightly more boring sister campus, purgatory. 'For every gold ducat that falls into the indulgence box another souls flies from purgatory,' was the advertising slogan that allowed the Medicis, Sforzas and Borgias to build empires on assassination and incest.

With self-appointed self-righteousness due to the hundreds of animals already saved from death over the past months, I felt that one small transgression could be made up for by penance. I couldn't give up alcohol. So I set myself the task of a further several months past the one-year deadline for giving up meat. I cleaned between my teeth with dental floss, which washed away the sins of the night before, and continued on my year and a half without meat.

I reduced and thickened the cooking juices of the lamb, to make a thin gravy. I chopped up several bunches of mint, mixed them with brown sugar and poured over some boiling hot water, to which I added a little vinegar, to make the mint sauce. I stripped the lamb from the bone in long morsels of muscle strands. At the party, after the paella was served and everyone was a little more boozy, I toasted some rolls, warmed the lamb and pressed it into the rolls, spooning over a good serve of gravy and mint sauce, salt and pepper, all wrapped in a paper napkin. I was told later just how good the lamb rolls were. Between two back molars nagged a muscle fibre that I had missed with the holy dental floss.

THAT EMAIL

Spring turned into summer. It was coming up to Christmas. The super-markets had put on their special Pavlovian spending music, formerly known as Christmas carols, and the ships stacked with containers of use-less-objects-later-to-be-given-as-gifts waited out on the bay for a berth to unload. I continued writing my column for *The Age Epicure*, called 'Brain Food'. This is a collection of single entendres and social commen-tary thinly veiled as a food and cooking question-and-answer column. A question had come in from a reader, an A Garfield, that seemed fes-tively consistent.

The query was a little long and needed editing to get to the nub of the question. It ended up reading: 'How do I cook the Christmas turkey so it doesn't end up dry? A Garfield'.

I replied:

You could consider one of the supermarket 'fresh whole' turkeys which contain 94 per cent turkey. Fancy that! The other 6 per cent contains diphosphates, polyphosphates, guar gum, xanthan gum, canola oil and sugar. Merry Christmas. Esteemed British food writer Matthew Fort gives a method that cooks the bird at 61°C–63°C for ten hours then finishes it with a blast of heat to brown the skin. Most ovens can't deliver such low temperatures accurately so it's not something I would recommend. The best turkey I ever had was cooked by my mate Macca. He took a free-range bird, not too big, and brined it in five litres of brine made with 2 cups of grey sea salt and a cup of raw sugar with half a dozen bay leaves, a small handful of fresh thyme and 6 crushed juniper berries which he simmered for 15 minutes and allowed to cool before putting in his turkey and keeping it overnight in the fridge. He roasted it in the normal manner. It was brilliant!

I felt this was quite a generous response and offered a good deal of information with a modicum of comment. I received several emails adding to the comments about supermarket food and suggesting other methods for brining and roasting a turkey. There was one email that stood out. I kept it. Here it is:

From: A cow <donteatme@youarseholes.com>

What gives YOU the right to KILL animals so you can stuff your fat arse?

I hope you come back as a pig … or a turkey … and get slaughtered inhumanely, like many animals do.

Pigs are very intelligent creatures—not that you'd give a fuck. Think about that this Christmas, cunt … and every other cunt that eats animals.

The 'restaurant industry' thinks it's ok to kill.

It isn't.

It reminded me that some do not see the consumption of meat as a subject for debate or a moral issue. They see it as war.

donteatme@youarseholes.com was, as you probably have guessed, a fake address.

I posted the email from A Cow as a mildly ironic Christmas greeting on social media. It received some comments, the best from one sharp friend who noted that the anonymous poster 'obviously and fundamentally misunderstands the basics of food consumption. Merry Christmas'.

MY MEAT-FREE CHRISTMAS

There are several smells that, when combined, signal to me that Christmas is around the corner. First, the smell of nutmeg, cinnamon and allspice. These are the three spices that my mother's maternal grandmother listed on the Christmas pudding recipe that she handed down to my mother. They are folded through a batter of egg, flour, milk, breadcrumbs, brown sugar and dried fruit: namely, raisins, currants, sultanas and mixed citrus peel that are soaked in brandy. This speckled sticky batter is spooned into greased pudding bowls, covered and gently simmered for four hours. They are generally cooked on one of those days bordering on subtropical that sweep through Victoria before the crap weather settles, spanning Christmas Eve to the week after New Year. Those spices always punch through the muggy air, painting the atmosphere with the aroma of anticipation.

There also needs to be the smell of pine needles. Pine needles and sap. We grew up on a farm where there were shelter belts of pine trees— rows of pine trees to create windbreaks for the sheep and cattle. The open woodland that had covered the country had been cut down and the stumps blasted sky high with TNT to create great swathes of green pasture. The seeds of the pine had blown into the remnant bush and lined the roadsides populating the stringybarks with sapling pine trees. We would eye them off in November, hoping no one from the neighbouring farms would have the same idea. The young tree, probably 2 metres tall, would have its lower limbs removed, its trunk shoved into a terracotta pipe, and would be stuck into a bucket that once contained some agricultural chemical but was now filled with water, and moved into the living room. The whole front of that weatherboard farmhouse would be filled with the clean, fresh aroma of pine tree.

Getting closer to the day, the excitement builds as the shortbread goes in the oven. Butter and flour in the hot oven create, with the risk of sounding synesthetic, a rich golden smell.

The aroma of roasting bird. When I wrote about Mum and Aunty Sue getting together to pluck chooks under the fragrant shade of the virgilia tree on Christmas Eve, there was something I didn't mention: a freshly killed chicken has the sweet smell of wet feathers, and when eviscerated, a pleasing rich smell. It's only when the chook is stuffed with breadcrumbs laced with onion fried in butter, lemon rind and fresh thyme leaves, then trussed up like a courtesan in a corset and sent into the scorching hot oven that the transubstantiation from backyard chook to Roast Chicken takes place. A Christmas miracle. There's an aroma released by chicken that is an olfactory clarion call to stop what you are doing, come inside, wash your hands, hover around the kitchen expectantly, be told off for picking at the pope's nose as the bird is being carved, sit hungrily at the table staring at the roast potatoes and wait for someone old to ask for grace to be said. That is the essential aroma of Christmas for me.

The table laden with meaty bounty is so much part of the Christmas tradition. Each meat speaks of a history of poverty and fast days. So when there was an excuse for a feast, meats proved you could afford to put bacon on the table. There needs to be ham from the pig fattened over autumn. As much red meat as one can muster and at least one type of poultry. In the Northern Hemisphere, goose is the most festive, as it is native and fattens naturally over autumn. Turkeys are relative newcomers, being only 400 years on the menu in Europe. Chicken, only becoming a cheap meat in the last generation, still holds cachet on the Christmas table.

A new baby in my partner's family saw us head to the country. For the past twenty years we had spent most Christmases with her great-grandmother. She was in her seventies when my partner and I first met, and a string of medical conditions meant that each Christmas could be her last. She loved ham and it was my job to get ham. One can't just buy some slices of ham from the deli and put them on the table. It has to be a ham. With the incredibly low cost of industrially raised pork and the way a ham can be mass-produced, that big celebratory Christmas item can be as low as $6.99 a kilo. You can put a decent-sized ham on the table to feed a cook's dozen and still get change out of $35. A ham that has been made from pork with all the ecological, ethical and human inputs considered will set you back $39 a kilo or about $200.

My partner's grandma lasted another twenty-two years. That's over $4000 worth of ham. It's not something that I like that much of, and find it very difficult to make leftover ham-based dishes. When she died, she did it with grace. 'I learned so many things in my life and now I am learning to die,' she said a few days before she passed away. I miss her.

But the second Christmas without her saw a new baby in the family. A beautiful second cousin called Audrey. Her parents are vegetarian and dinner was at their mother's house in the country.

It was one of those Victorian summer days when the clouds are like wool bales in the sky, and the grass not cut for hay is deep gold with a tinge of green about the bottom of the stem. It was slightly humid with the hint of a threat from the low pressure and the tops of some clouds going rampant, heading towards the stratosphere. Added to this was the tang of crushed eucalyptus leaves hanging in the air.

With the rugs spread under the poplar trees, the cicadas started their midday chorus. It is so much easier to prepare a Christmas lunch when you don't have to worry about roasting meat and vegetables for a dozen people in an oven designed to feed a nuclear family. It was also fun.

I normally make a terrine. This year I made a medieval gingerbread that is basically good-quality breadcrumbs, honey and dried ginger set in a tin. It has a meaty quality and is a perfect foil to goat's cheese and blue cheese.

A little cold asparagus soup, followed by a cauliflower mousse drizzled with a little salsa verde, and then a cheese and potato dish in homage to Jacques Reymond. (Finely slicing potatoes is never fun and is best done with a very sharp kitchen mandolin.) This dish was delicate enough to handle the verdelho but had enough oomph to work with the sparkling shiraz—something I love on Christmas Day.

You can blow off turkey, forget about ham, stuff your bloody chickens, but it is not Christmas without pudding. It was my intention prior to living through this Christmas to make it a vegan one. I wanted to call the chapter 'My Big Fat Vegan Christmas'. Christmas pudding is made with butter or suet (kidney fat) but there was no way I was going to go without pudding. It is the only day of the year you can put dried fruit, brandy, cream, custard and a sauce made with more brandy, and an emulsion of butter, sugar and more brandy, together on a plate with an old coin secreted somewhere in the dish for good luck. Bugger going vegan for Christmas.

15

Little Miracles

At the start of the following year, with very little warning, I found myself in Bali. An editor of a lifestyle magazine I work for had organised for me to interview a chef in Ubud. This is a town of 30 000 or so people in the foothills of the Balinese highlands. The entire town and its surrounding villages feel as if they have been carved from volcanic rock. Rock that has weathered under the tropical sun and torrential rain. Every house has a carved stone temple. Statues of the Hindu gods Ganesh, the elephant-headed god associated with new beginnings, and Hanuman, the monkey god, line the narrow, two-abreast-wide laneways that interlace the town and the surrounding villages.

Chef Nengah Suradnya met me with a professional handshake and enthusiastic smile. Born in Lombok he arrived in Sydney in the 1990s, just a week before the government clamped down on people applying for permanent residency. He found a job in the kitchen of the Park Hyatt Hotel in Canberra and worked his way up the restaurant kitchen brigade. Qualified and popular, he worked as a chef in other Canberra restaurants before buying his own bistro, which he named Element. He and his cooking were lauded by politicians and public servants, who appreciated his take on modern Australian cuisine. He left Australia in the early 2000s to explore his options across India and Indonesia, before settling in Penestanan, a beautiful village just south of Ubud.

Nengah's restaurant is open to the street and has the feel of a modern café in Surry Hills, Sydney, but a menu one would find in a local Toorak bistro. Nengah serves incredibly well-finessed and presented Western classics, such as confit duck leg, pork belly with cabbage, and grilled fish and risotto. It is known as the place where wealthy expats come for their comfort food when they are bored with nasi goreng and gado gado. Not that one would need to be wealthy, as the prices are one third of those one would pay in an Australian city restaurant. But it was Nengah's skill that really struck me. How did a boy from a Lombok village cook so well? When I asked him about his life journey as a chef, he also revealed why there is so much tension around the consumption of meat in our culture. After speaking with him it seemed bleedingly obvious, but the reason for this cultural dilemma had until then been hidden from me.

Nengah explained:

Men don't do the cooking at home but we cook when we are out fishing or hunting. The first time I cooked was when I was a boy. I was fishing with my father and I caught a fish. My father said to me, "Now it is your turn to cook it". I had seen him cook before. So I made a fire in the sand. Back then there was wild ginger and wild lemongrass growing in the forest next to the beach. I loved the elemental power of fire and the way it transforms the raw flesh into something completely different and delicious.

As a young man, Nengah went to work for his uncle, who had a small travel agency in Lombok in the 1980s. He guided Western tourists on treks 3000 metres up to the summit of Mount Rinjani. It was a long walk over several days in the tropical forest, and to keep food fresh, Nengah kept it alive.

Ooh, I had chickens and baby goat that we would take up with us. I would cut off the chicken's head and pluck and gut the chicken, and then light a fire and cook the rice and the chicken. Many of the Westerners had never seen an animal being killed before. When it came time to kill the baby goat there were people who pleaded with me not to kill it. They felt sorry for the animal. They would actually go hungry instead of letting me kill a young goat. But if I went away and killed the animals and cooked them, then they didn't feel sorry for the animal, so they would eat them. Even though they knew what I was doing. They pretended the slaughter wasn't happening. I learned a big lesson about Western people. Almost all of you have never seen an animal die. Fewer of you have ever killed one.

He poured me a powerful ginger martini and the discussion moved on.

With work done, I had most of the day to myself before the midnight flight back home. I was told that the first cremation in four years was being held in the village across the river. In the intervening four years the dead had been buried in a cemetery nearby and would be exhumed prior to their cremation. A concrete path snaked past villas, terraced rice paddies and *warungs*, through the forest and over the river to the main street. Stray brindle dogs nosed each other and hawker women insisted I buy a sarong as a mark of respect for the dead. There were twenty or so red-and-white life-size papier-mâché buffalo, known to the locals as *lembu*, standing on bamboo platforms lining the road. A small plaque on the front of each *lembu* denoted a deceased village person, many bearing the popular names Made and Kekut. They had been disinterred, dressed in fresh clothing, wrapped in fresh palm matting and laid out in the buffalo, as if they were sleeping.

It was late morning, the sun was hot and the village men were huddled in the shade. It wasn't a sad occasion. It was more like a small-town Easter parade where every person was taking part. Dressed in sarongs and commemorative T-shirts designating which local organisation they belonged to, they waited for the announcement over the village speakers. There was a call to action; they took their places and prepared to lift the buffalo with their loved ones inside onto their shoulders. Some of the buffalo were made with demonic spikes on their necks, virile and priapic. Others were more demure, with long eyelashes like the cow on La Vache Qui Rit French cheese packet. Drawings on cardboard on one side were filled with iconography of disembodied eyes, and what looked like a demon trying to turn a naked lady into a spit roast, using a rake handle. Not the type of decoration one would see at a Methodist send-off. The normal smell of rank water, clove cigarettes and durian was eclipsed by another, more decadent aroma. The smell of decaying people.

As part of the occasion, some small children climbed onto one of the platforms and the twenty or so papier-mâché buffalo were raised onto the men's shoulders and marched down to the site by the temple, where they were to be cremated. The children waved to the crowd. The drum band followed on, with twenty young men belting a rhythm on cymbals, sonorous bells and gongs. The procession meandered down the main street and the buffalo were lined up in rows. Offerings were made. More music was played. People looked to the sky for the auspices of the sun at its zenith. It was time to say goodbye. A solemnity overcame the crowd. The buffalo were lit by the families and the papier-mâché and fine wood quickly took the flames. Smoky at first, the breeze picked up the flames and within minutes they were ablaze. At one stage, a buffalo was completely engulfed in orange and black flames with only its head and strange bulging eyes emerging from the blaze. The heat was quite intense and the smoke circled around the square as the wind blew in up the valley. There was the aroma of wood smoke and charring flesh. The inferno was like Hieronymous Bosch had done some acid at Kuta before painting a quite hellish scene. The crowd watched. Some were praying. Some were wearing face masks and turning their heads away from the smoke and flames. The small children stood, looked and pointed. There was a flare-up and the belly of one of the *lembus* burned away to reveal a blackened bundle the size of what looked like a diminutive Balinese grandmother suspended within the framework of her burning sarcophagus. The fibres holding her in burned through and she dropped to the fiery platform headfirst. The legs of the fiery sarcophagus started to give way and very quietly the wooden buffalo twisted and folded down, collapsing in and around the body. The Balinese don't cry at these ceremonies. They are at this moment, however, allowed to shed a tear, to help their loved one on their journey to the next life. The children still looked on. They would see, hear and smell many more of these cremations in their lifetime.

Back in my hotel room I showered.

It was a wellbeing hotel, where the day started with yoga, coconut water and spirulina shakes. It was one of the few in Indonesia and possibly South-East Asia, that doesn't allow smoking. The menu was completely raw food.

This is a food movement. Eating raw food means that one mostly eats organic vegan food that has not been subjected to heat. One of the founding theories behind the movement is that heating food above 40 to 49 degrees Celsius destroys the enzymes that aid digestion. Adherents believe that raw food also contains microorganisms that aid the digestive tract by populating it with beneficial flora. Raw food advocates also maintain that cooking destroys nutrients in raw food. They also argue that cooked foods contain harmful toxins that can cause chronic disease. One of the major tenets of the movement is that raw food contains antioxidants that slow down ageing; it argues that processed food, tap water and air pollution are bad for you.

I sat down in the rooftop garden of the hotel, the late afternoon breeze picking up. I ordered a beer and a vegan raw-food tasting plate. As I waited I watched the scores of ragged fabric kites hovering in the breeze, tethered to playgrounds across Ubud. The fish, bird and fruit bat shapes were all edged in lots of loose cloth, making it look like we were under attack from a hundred colourful Dementors.

The food was very good. There was a 'burger' made with the folded inner leaves of an iceberg lettuce, cut to form crinkled cup shapes to represent buns. Inside were slices of tomato and onion and a thickened nut milk, flavoured with chilli. This came with grissini made with soaked grains and fine seeds that had been rolled into the grissini shape, dehydrated, and served with a paste made from crushed cashews and ripe, sweet red peppers.

It was really tasty food and I scribbled notes for some ideas for the home kitchen. In the back of my mind I couldn't help think about the dogma behind the food; I had surprisingly good Internet connection and download speed. Time for some research to debunk the raw food movement.

I was surprised to discover there is much merit in the teachings of the raw food movement. Diets high in foods containing anthocyanins have been associated with lower risks of cancer. Anthocyanins are the red-coloured compounds in food that cause beetroots and red wine grapes to be red. Raw food recipes call for lots of brightly coloured vegetables that contain these 'good for you' compounds. There are compounds in processed foods, such as the preservatives used in cured meats, that not only interfere with gut bacteria but also increase the risk of colon cancer (identified in studies by the World Health Organization). Some beneficial enzymes found in foods are destroyed at temperatures just above 40 degrees Celsius. One of the other concerns relates to something they refer to as excitotoxins in cooked and processed food that causes brain damage.

The last piece of information came as a surprise, as I thought excitotoxins were a made-up concept, like morgellons. (Morgellons are little fibres from an alien source that cause people to itch and scratch. While under the microscope they look like common garment fibres, some poor people think they are from outer space, sent to cause their skin to feel like hell.) Excitotoxins, however, exist. They are found mostly in the foods we find most delicious, and they enter the brain, where they cause damage to neurotransmitters. Some notable excitotoxins are glutamates that occur naturally in food, and are added to it in the form of MSG and other flavour enhancers. They rapidly destroy brain nerve cells by hyperactivating them. Another type of excitotoxin is domoic acid that is caused by red algae. In recent years some elderly people in Canada were killed by eating blue mussels that had fed on the toxic algae. It also affects other animals. Researchers attribute to domoic acid a highway incident in the United States in 2006 when a crazed California brown pelican flew through the windscreen of a car on the Pacific Coast Highway. The takeaway is this—don't feed your kids Twisties, or other junk food with MSG, and listen out for algae alerts.

So I would have to agree with most of what the raw foodatarians promote. There are swings and roundabouts when it comes to heating food. Some foods offer more nutrition when cooked. Mushrooms, for example, are more nutritious and offer more available potassium when cooked. Morels, a much-prized mushroom in Europe that can be found growing in the granite ranges of Victoria, are poisonous when raw but completely edible when cooked. The calcium, iron and magnesium in spinach are more available when cooked. Tomatoes contain a compound called lycopene, a carotenoid that has been identified as an antioxidant and is easier to absorb in cooked tomatoes. But in broccoli the myrosinase, the enzyme that helps break down compounds in the liver, is destroyed when heated.

Heating food destroys bad microbes. But cooking food at high temperatures creates acrylamides. Acrylamides have been associated with cancer in laboratory rats. You'll find acrylamides in fried or roasted potato products, coffee, and cereal-based products, including sweet biscuits and toasted bread. So, raw food lovers do have some really good points to make.

But what I found annoying and off-putting was the way the raw food argument is often couched in a passive-aggressive tone, something like this:

> Your body is actually sort of an alkaline battery, running on electrons. All life-giving chemical reactions only happen when electrons or energy flows between atoms. Cooking or processing causes food to lose electrons—the source of the energy your body needs. Things that are healthy 'contribute' electrons/energy, and are called alkalising or 'reducing'. Things that are unhealthy steal electrons/energy, and are called acidic or 'oxidising' (which means to burn up, rust, break down or decay). Your body is designed to be alkaline, like the battery!

It is interesting to watch a new food movement form. Unsure of themselves and eager to please, advocates of raw food are creating food analogues, dishes that replicate the concept of an existing and accepted format. The raw version of cooked food, the binary opposite of the norm; take an existing food and make a raw version of it. It's like building props from papier-mâché. It's the same sad path that some vegetarians went down by creating meat-free versions of the real thing. The logic behind an industrial vegetarian product like Tofurky—tofu turkey—is that it is the fake copying the 'real' version. While the raw food movement is still in the phase of trying to prove itself, it could possibly overcome this misstep. Hopefully, it will forge its own path, and create some interesting food that celebrates the flavour of truly excellent fruit and vegetables.

I flew back to Melbourne on one of those hot days when the wind blows down from the north. A hot, dry wind that seems to pick up every different type of pollen, dust and tiny irritating granule of matter from the parched interior, and funnel it into one's eyes, nose and throat. As a long-time sufferer of hay fever, these are the days I dread most. A blocked nose that can erupt into a streaming mass of ectoplasmic mucus in the blink of an eye. A roof of the mouth that itches incessantly. Eyes that feel like tiny ants are crawling around the sides of them. Sneezing attacks that last for minutes, rendering one unable to talk, walk or, even worse, drive. I walked outside the airport through a wall of cigarette smoke produced by ashen-faced travellers. A small eddy of wind picked up a pile of dead leaves, dust and boarding passes and threw it in my face. I did not sneeze, I did not twitch, I did not wheeze, I did not itch. I did not get hay fever.

Meat contains a substance called arachidonic acid. I did not research this until my hay fever stopped. To me arachidonic acid sounds like something you'd get if you put spiders in a grape press. It is structurally related to arachidic acid, found in peanut oil. (*Arachis hypogaea* is the botanical name for the peanut plant.) Arachidonic acid is a fatty acid and is important in the functioning of our bodies, doing a range of jobs, such as getting certain cells to go about their tasks—that's called cellular signalling. It helps get certain enzymes up and running to do their chores in the body. It is a vasodilator—meaning it widens blood vessels. It also plays an important part in our body's inflammatory response.

In the early 2010s, respected human nutrition researcher Dr Richard Rosenkranz, working at the University of Western Sydney, undertook a cross-sectional study of 156,035 Australian men and women. He found that high meat consumption was associated with a 25 per cent increase in diagnosed hay fever or asthma, and a 10 per cent increase in asthma alone. In an article detailing the study's findings, published in 2012 in *Nutrition Journal*, he concluded:

> Generally, diets marked by greater intakes of meats, poultry, and seafood were associated with diagnosed asthma and hay fever. Taken together, these findings suggest that adherence to a more meat-based diet may pose risk for asthma and asthma/hay fever in Australian adults. The research also explored that a typical

Western diet is poor in antioxidants and high in saturated fats that makes the people susceptible for these ailments.

After a lifetime of suffering a face explosion every time the wind changed, I no longer had hay fever. A diet of really good seasonal vegetables and grains had put an end to over four decades of never feeling safe to leave the house unless I had several handkerchiefs stuffed into my pockets and a spare pack of tissues lying in my laptop bag.

I also lost weight. Lots of weight. As I said before, I am not a small man. But after nearly twelve months without eating meat (except for some notable transgressions) I was substantially smaller. When I first spoke to the editor of *The Age Epicure* about writing on this topic, I weighed 120 kilograms. That's about two washing machines. When I stepped onto the scales a year later I weighed 103 kilograms. I had been walking around with the equivalent of a well-built blue heeler around my waist for almost a decade. This weight loss made my knees very happy. I suffer from a degenerative bone disease (nothing serious, you don't need to organise a crowd-funded charity bike marathon for me), which makes my knees hurt. Weighing less means they hurt less.

It was time for the doctor's appointment. Again, nothing serious, just the ritual sitting down and being told off for drinking too much and being too fat, by someone who drives a considerably better car than I ever will. I also had my blood tested to see how my iron levels were going. I knew I was healthier but it's not something you can put a number on. It's not often I get praise from my GP. It's not often that I leave the doctor's rooms feeling emotionally better. But on this day I walked out the door feeling taller, lighter, fitter and healthier. My cholesterol was down from seven to five. He told me the lower the number, the better. I believed him. He drives an Audi S4.

16

The Loneliest Vegetarian in Andalusia

The flight attendant ushered me to the left. I took my seat and played with the seat controls, like an 8-year-old boy. I made the seat lie flat then bend in the middle, before quickly bringing it to upright position as the cabin crew started pouring the champagne. I have the best job in the world. I travel across Australia and around the world writing about food. On this occasion, my work with MoVida group of restaurants saw MoVida chef and co-owner Frank Camorra and me heading back to Spain for another book. We were flying Turkish Airlines, as they fly into Málaga from Singapore. We were up the pointy end of the plane, thanks to a favour from our mates at the Spain Tourism office in Singapore. Turkish Airlines prides itself on its food and has an onboard chef plating up meals for business class. Once the passengers were seated, the chef, wearing a large, soft beret, entered the cabin with a theatrical flourish. It was impressive but still quite absurd, as airlines use the same airport caterers. He was garnish.

I have always ordered vegetarian meals when flying. Not due to health concerns. Quite the opposite. 'Special' meals are delivered before the main meal drop, so you get the flight attendant wandering around the aisle trying to match the seat number on the sticker on the meal with your seat number on the display above the seat. You get served first and get a glass of wine before the rest of the cabin. On long-haul flights you can be fed and watered, wrapped up in the thin synthetic blanket and have your eyeshades on while the rest of the plane is still grinding their way through their chicken in grey sauce.

The meal was good. A really well-presented, inoffensive pan-global vegetable dish, showing off some good knife skills in carving the veg; a nod to Turkey's Mediterranean culinary heritage and a decent feed. This was followed by French cheese, Turkish pastries and good coffee. Excellent. Because I was heading to Spain, a nation where vegetarianism is still in its conceptual phase, I realised it would probably be the last time I would easily get a meat-free meal.

A NANO-HiSTORY OF SPAiN AND iTS LOVE OF PORK

Spaniards eat a lot of meat. The average Spaniard consumes 118 kilograms of flesh each year, a 6-fold increase since the dark days of the Franco era, when they existed mostly on seasonal vegetables and around 50 grams of meat per day. Today, Spaniards eat over 300 grams of meat a day. Their industrially raised chicken is really good compared with the bland $10 chicken we see here. But travellers to Spain don't see much chicken in restaurants, as it is considered food for the home. In the centre and north of the country, Spaniards also eat a lot of lamb, and game in season, and throughout the country seafood, jamón and pork appear in almost every dish. And I mean every dish. There's a great vegetable dish called *menestra*—seasonal veg of perhaps runner beans and squash, sometimes cooked in a little tomato sauce. Various versions are made across the country, perhaps with more tomato in the south and more beans in the north. What unites them is not just the seasonal nature of the dish but the use of jamón. Jamón in Spain is not just air-dried ham. It is not the Spanish equivalent of prosciutto; it is much more than that. Eating jamón is a patriotic act, something one does when one is truly Spanish. This has its roots in the fifteenth century, when publicly eating pork was a culinary shibboleth, a tacit act to prove to everyone watching that one was neither a Muslim nor a Jew.

When the Moors crossed the Mediterranean from North Africa into the Iberian Peninsula in the early 700s, pork was well and truly on the menu. Previous invaders, the Romans, had already established a trade in ham, sending back to Rome pork preserved in lard in terracotta amphorae. As the Roman Empire in the west fell, the Visigoth rulers filled the vacuum. Within a few centuries the Visigoths were at war with each other, leaving them vulnerable to the expanding Muslim caliphate that was sweeping out of the Middle East and around the African shores of the Mediterranean. In 712 a Berber called Tariq ibn Ziyad landed near Gibraltar and marched north towards where Jerez de la Frontera is today. His troops defeated Visigoth king Roderic at the Battle of Guadalete and then marched north, eventually taking over almost all of the Iberian Peninsula, stopping at the Picos de Europa and leaving the Christian Kingdom of Asturias on the green coast of the Bay of Biscay intact. For most of the 780 years of Muslim rule in the Iberian Peninsula, Jews and Christians were allowed to remain and still practise their religions, as long as they paid the *jizyah*, or tax. Jews and Christians are considered 'People of the Book' according to the Qur'an, and are allowed to live in conquered lands as long as they pay the *jizyah* and 'feel themselves subdued'.

The Christian kings of the north were less convivial towards the Muslims as they slowly reconquered Spain, slaughtering many of them as they regained territory. The Jews too were massacred, with tens of thousands killed in genocides in cities across Spain. The reconquest of Spain, however, also saw Jews and Muslims offered the possibility of converting to Christianity. Those who did became *conversos*. Becoming a *converso* meant more than being baptised. The reality was Jews and Muslims were worshipping Christ and eating pork in public but praying to Yahweh or Allah in secret.

There is a groundswell of Jewish academics believing that one of Spain's greatest and most memorable literary characters was a *converso*. In Miguel de Cervantes' *Don Quixote*, the sidekick, Sancho Panza, describes himself as an 'old Christian' while the Don Quixote just says that he is a Christian. In one chapter, Quixote's food is described as '*una olla de algo más vaca que carnero, salpicón las más noches, duelos y quebrantos los sábados, lantejas los viernes, algún palomino de añadidura los domingos*'. This refers to such dishes as a stockpot with beef or chopped mutton. *Salpicón* is salad, which is eaten most nights; he eats lentils on Fridays, and on Sundays he has some squab—a dish showing his pretensions to nobility. Notice, however, there is no pork. Except a dish called '*duelos y quebrantos*'. This was a dish of eggs cooked in pork fat, with other porky bits, and eaten by *conversos* in public on the Jewish Sabbath and to break the laws of kashrut to prove that one was not a Jew. Chewing the fat to save one's neck. *Conversos* went to elaborate lengths to prove their newfound obedience to the Catholic Church and, more importantly, the Catholic kings of Spain. Cured hams would hang in kitchens, where they could be seen by the outside world.

The foods of the Moors and Sephardic Jews are still cooked in the kitchens of Christian Spaniards today. Dishes such as lamb roasted with honey, and fish balls made with minced fish and stale breadcrumbs. While these dishes are largely eaten in the south, pork and jamón are ubiquitous across the peninsula. From the fat rendered from chorizos spread on toasted bread at breakfast, to the lard used in pastries made in convents, to the chunks of pork and jamón that sit in legume stews such as *cocido* and *fabada*, pork is king in Spain. Long live the king.

Asking for a meal without meat in Spain is greeted not with contempt but puzzlement. 'Why would you not eat meat?' is asked politely. This attitude comes from a people for whom starvation during the Spanish Civil War is still within their living memory. Thousands died from want of food. Countless thousands more fled to the hills and lived on food foraged from the wild. This plays out today with a craze for fungus in the wealthier north of the country, particularly among the Gen Xers and younger people. In the south there is still resistance, particularly from older people, who associate eating mushrooms with the hard years of the Spanish Civil War.

This understanding of poverty has resulted in food waste being a non-existent problem in the traditional kitchens of the south, where there is a use for anything that is edible. This sees tiny bits of jamón, such as the bone and the skin, used in dishes to create flavour, texture and nutrition. This also sees every single part of the pig, as well, used in the kitchen after slaughter. In a bar in Extremadura, several years before this visit, I was served a tapa plate of pickled pigs' tails sprinkled with local smoked paprika. That was it. Pickled pigs' tails. In Calle de la Cruz in Madrid, there is a bar that specialises in flat grilled pigs' ears and sweetbreads called La Oreja de Jaime. In Australia we'd call it 'Jamie's Ears'.

Breakfast for a vegetarian in Spain is easy. It's generally coffee, freshly squeezed orange juice and perhaps some toast and jam. Depending on what you did the night before, the juice and toast can be substituted with a cigarette and brandy. If you want *manteca*, rendered sausage fat, you can have it on toast. Or you can also have fresh tomato pulp, salt and extra virgin olive oil on toast, if you like. If you're staying in a hotel with a dining room, then order the *revueltos*. These are like scrambled eggs but eight times better. Slightly wet and silky they are often enriched with *hongos* or *setas*, known in English as mushrooms. With coffee and juice, *reveultos con setas* sets the day up beautifully.

When we landed on this trip it was early spring and the first of the artichokes and asparagus were in the markets. This made eating meat-free a lot easier as they were specials on most menus. Artichokes cooked in sherry is a popular dish, although jamón is often added to the dish. The port city of Málaga is known for its *porras*, thick cold soups made with bread, and a cousin of gazpacho. The recipes for these dishes are thousands of years old, mentioned in the Old Testament, and the dishes are still eaten on a daily basis. They could be made with oranges; perhaps tomatoes or garlic. We found in Marbella a dish of eggs stuffed with piquillo peppers and slathered in mayonnaise, a fragrantly spicy dish of spinach with chickpeas and pine nuts, plus desserts with sponge and cream. The south of Spain is also home to a diverse range of sheep's and goat's milk cheeses, some raw milk and semi-matured, making them very deep flavoured and delicious. There is also a new breed of bakers in the south of Spain who are supplanting the Franco-era dry industrial white breads with really good-quality long-time fermented bread.

EL MATACHIN

After some time spent on the sunny Mediterranean we were heading up to the region of Huelva. We were driving there to explore the lore around *la matanza*, or the killing of the pig, and to speak with the maker of one of the best jamóns in the nation. Huelva is to the north-west of Seville. One way of getting there is to go down to the coast near Cádiz, then follow the shore north towards Portugal. This route more or less follows the meandering estuary of the Guadalquivir, or Great River. Literally. *'Guadal'* is Arabic for river and *'quivir'* means great. It rises in the Sierra de Cazorla and flows through Córdoba and Seville, before making its way through the plains to the Atlantic at Sanlúcar de Barrameda. Dotted on the plains are towns with names like Isla Mayor or 'biggest island'. The area was once a waterworld, a massive wetland, the Kakadu of Europe. It was home to an ancient civilisation called the Tartessos, who navigated between the islands in boats. They had their own language, currency and culture. When the wetlands began to be drained by the Phoenicians for salt farming and aquaculture, the Tartessos were vulnerable and their civilisation died out. This vast wetland was slowly diminished over the millennia, river flows slowed and the delta it fed silted up, creating a brand new coast around Cádiz. The final straw came with Franco, who turned over vast areas to rice farming. One of the planet's great wetlands was transformed into farmland. When we talk about the effects that agriculture has on the environment, you only need look at what is left of the Guadalquivir delta. There are remnants, amazingly, of what once covered a sixth of Andalusia. In the Doñana National Park flamingos sieve for krill in the briny lagoons, while kites reel in the sky above. Hares lope about the scrub on the dunes, while schools of young fish break the surface of the still waters in a silvery shimmer. There is a drainage channel, and then flat rice fields to the horizon in every direction for 180 degrees.

Huelva is a place that the rest of Spain jokes is backward. As Wales is to England. Tasmania to mainland Australia. And like Wales and Tasmania, the prejudice towards this region is matched by the beautiful reality, and the open-mindedness of the inhabitants that is misinterpreted by outsiders as naivety or backwardness. Apart from a few mining scars from the Rio Tinto mines and an as-yet-not-overdeveloped coastline, much of the region is sierra covered in forest.

The Sierra de Aracena is some of the most beautiful and bucolic landscape in Spain. Roads carved from the hillside, long before cars, are so narrow that you have to slow down. They rise along ridges to reveal green mountain valleys covered in forests of cork oak, holm oak, chestnut and fragrant scrub. The roads drop into the valley floors where clearings have been made for small farms. The fences are dry stone, and in the shade of ancient oak, lay cattle. Nestled in a saddle between two small mountains is the town of Linares de la Sierra. It is a white stone village separated from the forest by a snaking stream. On its flood plains are the *huertas* or kitchen gardens. Beyond the *huertas* is *la dehesa*, a massive swathe of forest that covers 2.5 million hectares of south-west Spain and eastern Portugal. A lot of it has been declared parkland.

To think of it like a national park would be wrong. While almost no commercial activity is allowed in a national park, the forest around Linares de la Sierra, and much of this part of the world, has been farmed for centuries. In Spain this process is called *la ganadería*, in which animals are raised in the outdoors. Think shepherds protecting and moving their flocks. In some parts of the country, great flocks of sheep are herded across large distances, including through the heart of towns and villages in *la trashumancia*. The forest around Linares de la Sierra is the foraging grounds for the village's pigs. The pigs are fed grain and scraps, and so return to their feeding spot daily. However, they are free to roam the oak and chestnut forest during the rest of the day, eating the autumn fall of nutrient-rich acorns and chestnuts as well as feeding on grasses, insects and the worms and tubers they find as they root about in the earth.

They are large black pigs. They are not the famous Iberico pigs used for making jamón. They are mongrel pigs that over the years have been bred to suit the local conditions. The locals just call them *autóctono* or autochthonous. All the town's pigs are slaughtered by just one man. He is the town's *matachín*. It is a role that is passed down through the town's men.

We met with Juan Marquez, who was Linares de la Sierra's *matachín* for many decades. His granddaughter Laura welcomed us into his home, settled us into chairs and went to fetch her grandfather. The thick stonewalled cottage had been renovated in recent years, the walls lined with plaster and the old roof covered with a plaster ceiling. There were photographs on the wall of Juan as a handsome young man with sweeping black hair and sporting a broad-shouldered suit. The slim woman next to him in the photos was presumably Laura's grandmother, for they both had the same slim waist, round hips, long but refined nose, and full lips wearing the same smile. Juan was now old and almost completely deaf. He came in and was helped into his chair by Laura. He was warm and welcoming but seemed perplexed as to why we had come from so far away to learn about his time as the town *matachín*. Not bewildered. Interested. We paid our dues, showed our respect, and explained our mission to learn about the annual killing of the pig and making the jamóns and sausages. Juan seemed comfortable with our explanation and began to tell his story.

'I killed my first pig when I was still quite young,' he began, sitting upright and pleased but not proud to have an attentive audience.

It was always a busy time in the village and something we all looked forward to. There was always so much to be done. So much work and preparation. Washing of tools and gathering of wood. All the boys in the village would crowd around the *matachín* when he stuck the pig. We would watch the pig as the blood flowed out and someone caught it in a pan. I never knew a pig had so much blood inside him. I would help cut the pig in two. Here in Linares we don't [until recently] have modern chillers, so we still cool our pigs on the cold stone pavers that line the village streets. The old *matachin* saw I was taking great interest but was not as gruesome as the other boys. Then one day, when I was fourteen, he took me aside and quietly said, 'Now it is your turn'.

For Juan this was a grave duty. He was responsible not just for dispatching the town's pigs but for doing so in a suitable manner. Almost all of the meat from the pigs would be turned into sausages: chorizo, morcon and morcilla. The legs would be made into jamóns. A pig that dies well will leave a body still full of muscle sugar (glycogen) that is turned into lactic acid during fermentation, in the case of producing sausages, or by enzymes when producing jamón. A nice acidic sausage or jamón resists bacterial attack as it dries. When a sausage or jamón is dry it is shelf stable and can safely last for years if stored correctly. The calmer the pig is at its death the better the quality of the sausage. If a pig is terrified at its death it uses all its muscle sugar trying to escape. The meat won't ferment as well and there is a greater chance the sausages will spoil.

Resting his hand over his heart, Juan said:

I love animals. I really love them. I love my friends and family too. More. It was my responsibility not only to provide families with meat and smallgoods to feed them over the long cold winters, but I was also chosen to be the one person in the village to make sure the pigs did not needlessly suffer. The other young men did not have the steady hand. They were too bloodthirsty. The pig would look into their eyes and know they had death on their mind.

I don't know if his eyes were just rheumy but there were little tears forming in their corners. Laura held his hand.

The words 'the pig would look into their eyes' struck me. There was another pig I remember. It looked me in the eye. His name was Gub-Gub. He was the pig I raised for the family Christmas dinner. I, like Juan had been, was fourteen. I bought Gub-Gub as a piglet from a neighbour and named him after the pig in *Doctor Dolittle*, one of the first animals with whom the lead character in the 1967 film learned to talk. Gub-Gub was small and black. He liked his back scratched and to chase chickens. He in turn was chased by the cows. He loved mud, grass, warm wheatmeal and plastic pots. On our neighbouring farm lived a Bavarian butcher who spent his weekend mornings killing animals and turning them into leberkäse, landjäger, and bloodwurst. He was a fine butcher, who had his own high-speed mincing machine that looked like a torture device from an early James Bond film. He had a recipe for every part of the animal and would sing when slaughtering and yodel when smoking his sausages. With limited English and a voice like gravel he warned me early on, between puffs from his hand-rolled cigarette, that 'A pig is not a pet. For both of your sakes, do not let it become your friend.'

Christmas drew near and the pig got fatter. I fed him warm pollard and grains, and scraps from the kitchen. I'd scratch his back and he'd grunt contentedly. He'd follow me around the yard and I would throw him weeds over the fence as I tended the vegetable garden. He'd play with them and throw them back, like a dog with a stick.

One day, Gub-Gub followed me over to my neighbour's. I had already been there earlier in the morning, filling an old bathtub with water and lighting a gas burner under it. Hot water removes the hair from a pig. Pigs have a funny gait, as if their hips were not finished properly when they were invented. Gub-Gub walked over the paddocks, stopping to root around in a particularly rich patch of weeds, then gingerly approached the gravel driveway. He didn't like gravel on his trotters.

Gub-Gub followed me into the old dairy where my neighbour did his killing. The butcher looked at neither of us. He went about his preparations like a dentist going through his array of scrapers, sticks and mirrors. He sharpened one particularly worn knife. It had a thin curved blade and dark wooden handle. He took a rope, looped it a few times around itself to create a noose, and in one deft movement had Gub-Gub the pig hogtied. 'Hold this under the knife,' he said, passing me a shallow enamel dish. He took the knife and pushed it into Gub-Gub's neck. He didn't just slice, he gouged it around to open up the wound to let more blood flow. Gub-Gub squealed in terror. The dying pig fought against the rope and squealed again. He looked me in the eye, then his eyes saw nothing. That look of betrayal is something I carry with me always.

The bell rang out across the village. Laura placed her hand on her grandfather's shoulder. Our time with him was up; they had a priest to listen to. 'Because every death is different so every carcass must be prepared differently,' said Juan. 'I was the *matachín* and I was followed by the *gandinguera*.' She is the guardian of the traditional recipes. Juan told us that she would help the families on the day of the *matanza*. 'She would take a little sample of their sausage mixture, *la preuba*,' he explained, 'and fried it. She would taste it and suggest more salt, less pepper, more smoked paprika, less thyme.' Those ingredients contain different bacteria-retarding compounds and the amount of salt can alter the fermentation of the sausages. Complex food science that was determined by taste, not probes.

'*La matanza* was always considered a festive day,' continued Juan. 'All the village had so much fun. Except for the pig.'

THE TEMPTATION OF JAMÓN

The following day we travelled to the small town of Corteconcepción. We were there to find the Eiriz family of jamón makers. We had instructions to head to the town laundry and that the factory would be opposite that. We stopped a builder and asked directions, and he pointed towards the village centre. Very quickly the road gave way to old mule track. We parked the car and walked. The mule track narrowed to a 2-abreast walking path. We followed the directions from old women, perplexed to see a group of grown men heading to the town laundry. The laundry was outdoors. A long stone trough with well-worn corrugations either side was fed from the spring under the village. This is where women still brought their washing and scrubbed it in the running water. Several cobbled lanes verged on the washing well, the lanes lined with 2- and 3-storied white stone buildings, built sometime in the 1700s, some leaning more precariously over the lane than the others. None of them looked like a factory. It was the grunting of pigs and the braying of a lone donkey that led us to the last building opposite the laundry. There in the paddock, standing next to an old tractor, were a donkey and a middle-aged man. Judging by the way he was scratching it behind the ears and talking to it in the tone and inflection usually saved for the neonatal, the donkey was more pet than beast of burden. On the hill behind the two was a small herd of pigs lying in the sun by a small dam near the oak forest. 'Where's the jamón factory?' we called out. 'Behind you. Look for the sign of the smiling pig,' he called across the paddock as he petted his donkey.

Almost everywhere people eat pork they advertise it with a picture of a happy pig. Not just a normal-looking pig but a pig that is enthusiastically happy about being turned into ham or that has been anthropomorphised so much that you could be forgiven for thinking you were eating human flesh. When I was growing up, my father would drive us to the Dandenong Market to sell dairy calves. Dandenong was also home to The Dandenong Ham and Bacon Factory, makers of Dandy Hams. The pig that advertised the ham made from his fellow species was dressed in top hat and tails, waistcoat, striped trousers and two-tone shoes, with a cane under one arm, sported a monocle and stood joyously upright. So happy was he to see us that he doffed his top hat in a 3-motion neon animation. The pig at Jamónes Eiriz was simply smiling like a blissfully ignorant pork loon.

Domingo Eiriz is the sixth generation in his family to make jamón. He is the youngest son, gregarious, social and professional. His older brother, Manuel, the one with the pet donkey, worked on the factory floor. His other brother did other work somewhere else in the plant. Domingo led us through it. It had a modern skin of insulated aluminium, approved by the European Union health department, slipped inside to line the historic building. He explained that the pigs on the hill were 'representative' of the way pigs were raised in *la dehesa*. Kind of like a

Truman Show for pigs. All the pigs for his factory are raised around the area, and sent away to be slaughtered and dismembered in another town that has the abattoirs. The bits are trucked to the factory in this little town of 600 or so, and reassembled and given another life as *embutidos y jamones*. Smallgoods and jamón.

The first part of the process had not changed much since the 1960s. There were still rows of women stuffing spiced and salted pork flesh and fat into sausage skins made from the cleaned entrails of pigs, which were then sewn and strung up and sent off to be fermented. This was the fate of the bits of the pig that cannot be cured into jamón or paleta (jamón is the cured back leg, paleta is the front leg). Great strings of intestines unravelled from buckets to tie off the chorizo and morcon. It was not dissimilar to a photograph in a 1970 Time Life book I have called *The Cooking of Spain and Portugal*. The modern scene was just better lit and the women weren't smoking. The whole room was filled with the smell of garlic and smoky paprika.

Domingo led us through the sausage drying rooms with their forest of *lomos*, strips of loin muscles, hanging from racks. We walked towards the inner sanctum, *los secaderos de jamón*—the jamón drying rooms. We ducked as we entered a low-domed-ceiling room, open to the outside world through shuttered windows. We gasped and uttered words of amazement but the sound disappeared, absorbed by the irregular shapes of the hundreds of jamóns hanging silently from the ceiling. Their flesh was wine red, their skins gouda yellow, all decked with dark spots and patches of grey-and-white mould. These were two years old. They were some of the best hams made in Europe. Deeper tasting and considered more masculine than the pinker prosciutti of Parma, these would sell for many hundreds of euros across Spain and around the rest of Europe.

'You must understand that making jamón is a very special process,' said Domingo. 'It is a battle defending the jamón from the putrefying bacteria by curing it with salt and drying it in the mountain air. At the same time we are also creating a fertile place for the beneficial moulds and enzymes that transform the meat proteins into very delicious salt crystals that embed the flesh,' he continued in wonderfully considered English. Like many Spaniards, he had done the summertime food trade shows in the United States and twanged his 'r's like an American. 'Basically jamón sits some-where between mummification and transubstantiation. It is a miracle.'

The jamón *secaderos* were truly beautiful. The jamóns themselves created an irregular surface that followed the contours of the building, making it look and sound as if a recording studio had been created by a meat-loving acoustic engineer. While the flesh soaked up the sound of our voices and leather boots on hard cold stone, the jamóns themselves exuded an aroma that was a mix of mushroom, camembert cheese, dried meat, sweet flesh, and a word I learned working in Scottish pub cellars when I was in my early twenties—fusty.

Domingo finished the tour by taking us to the old house. There were pot plants and mops and other clues that this was a real house and not just a showroom. You find this often in Spain where you're taken to try food in what seems like an old-fashioned country village home or farmhouse but is in fact only used as display centre; the family has headed into the comfort of a nearby town or city, or even Madrid or Barcelona, leaving the old family home as a piece of corporate theatre.

Domingo leveraged a jamón into the oak *jamoneria*, the cradle that holds the jamón as one cuts it. In Spain the jamón cutter is the *cortador*. Add '*dor*' or '*ista*' at the end of a root word and you get a profession. *Matador, barista*. A *cortador* '*corts*' or cuts jamón for a living. In Italy they are called *violinieri*. The prosciutto cutter holds the ham like a violin, ankle in the hand, butt under the chin, the sharp thin blade cutting back and forward over the fret-like femur as if it were a Stradivarius. Sometimes the *violinieri* misjudges the resistance of muscle or nicks a bone and the mis-angled blade of his knife flies into his nose. Most *violinieri* have a nose many NRL players would recognise. The Spanish are less flamboyant and rely on the slightly safer *jamoneria*.

Go almost anywhere in Australia and ask the deli manager for prosciutto and they will finely slice it into ultra-thin slices. This is excellent when draped over a piece of sweet ripe melon or loosely wrapped around a grissini or layered across a pizza. This allows maximum surface area of the prosciutto to be exposed to the air in the mouth. Warmed by the heat of the tongue the aromatics in the fat and flesh are liberated, sending pillows of meaty fragrance up over the back of the mouth into the back of the nose—the retro-nasal part of our head, which is where we smell.

The mistake often made with fine smallgoods such as prosciutto and jamón is caterers rolling the paper-thin slices into rosettes. These we chew into a pulp, missing the point, and the experience of the delicate texture and complex aroma.

The Spanish have solved this problem by cutting their jamón into *lonchas*—roughly the shape of a matchbox and the thickness of a summer power bill. A *loncha* fits perfectly on the tongue. It is perhaps the best-designed shape on the planet for delivering the flavour of aged dried ham from the tongue into the olfactory centre.

With his long round-ended blade, fine like a fish knife, Domingo delicately cut into a 3-year-old jamón. The old kitchen—made of stone, with dark oak beams supporting the white roof, not decorated but lined with old (no, arcane) cooking implements—was filled with the aroma of some of the best sliced ham on the planet. Nuts, sweet old flesh, mushrooms. Frank Camorra was waiting quietly to one side. Cesc Castro, our researcher and great friend, was hovering nearby. He is Catalan and, by birth, should be immune to the seductive powers of Andalusian jamón. Our photographer and another good friend, Alan Benson, was quietly taking his images. I watched both of them. They were oscillating closer and closer to the plate that Domingo was preparing for us to shoot.

The sweet, fleshy aroma was truly beautiful. Australians, like me, use the word 'beautiful' to describe the things that attract us. We use the word to describe things that are more than visual. Beautiful for us means a scenic vista, an attractive setting, an agreeable coalescence of otherwise random events, a person with an outrageously attractive body, the intake on the bonnet of a Ford Falcon from the late sixties. We Australians apply the word beautiful very easily. This jamón was beautiful to all senses.

I was watching Frank eat jamón. He loved it. He was holding the *lonchas* gently, his thumb and forefinger pinched, and raised it above his mouth. He angled his head slightly and laid the jamón on his tongue. He chewed a little, smiled and nodded approvingly to Domingo. Domingo smiled too. He knows the effect his jamón has on people.

He passed the plate around. Cesc and Alan repeated the process. Cesc gave a wry half-smile and nodded. Great praise from a Catalan. Alan took a piece, chewed, smiled and nodded his head from side to side as he chewed and tasted. 'Good,' he said. 'Excellent.' Domingo passed the plate to me. He didn't understand that when I held up a hand I was suggesting that he pass it back to Frank. He pushed it forward. The fat was creamy white. '*Come*', he said, 'eat'. The flesh was ruby red. 'Try some.' I could smell nuts and mushrooms rising from the plate. 'It's good,' he said. There were small white salt crystals in the flesh that I knew would crunch between my teeth and release a wave of umami. 'You must,' said Domingo. The ribbon of fat was as wide as a butterknife, the *loncha* as thick as a communion wafer. The fat seemed to draw the heat from my tongue, like a tablet of excellent chocolate. The aroma was subtle yet complex, like perfume applied in the morning worn well into the afternoon. Faded roses, forest floor, champignons, a punch of pork, aged pork, and oak, something decayed but in the best possible way. This was held together by a backbone of salt, a clean lactic tang, and round and lingering savouriness. It was possibly the best piece of flesh I had ever eaten. In a rapid piece of self-reconciliation I knew that my time of penance and refection was over. That jamón was a work of art. I had crossed a threshold and there was no going back. My Year Without Meat closed with a single *loncha* of jamón ibérico de bellota.

17

Return to Meat

Food is simply the vehicle to write about everything else that goes on in the world. It is a Trojan Horse that not only gets food writers such as myself through the front gates undetected, but sees someone take your coat, and offer you a glass of sparkling wine and canapés on the way in. Talking about food with strangers allows one to assemble an almost complete and frank biography of the interlocutor as they talk about their family, hometown or village, parents and siblings, lovers and travels. They are talking about two things they really love talking about, themselves and food.

On that trip to Spain we met an ex-cop and his wife who had a restaurant high in the mountains of Sierra de Cazorla, the source of the Guadalquivir. He shot the game and she cooked it. They presented one dish of *andrajos*, meaning 'rags'. It is a hearty dish of hand-rolled pasta served with a simple sauce of beans and red peppers, and in this case a little slow-cooked hare. While the red peppers are a sixteenth-century post-Columbian addition, there is a version made at Easter without the pepper, with just vegetables and lentils. It is a dish that a well-fed centurion in the Roman Hispanian legion would have recognised some 2000 years ago and is described in the writings of Roman scholars. When I find a new dish I compare it with all the dishes I have learned about in the past. Each bit of information interconnects with another. You can almost feel the synapses joining up every time you learn about a new dish. That is the joy of learning.

We had finished our Spanish research and photography. The team had spent over a month in a small BMW and driven more than 10 000 kilometres. At one point, Cesc the researcher had backed the BMW into a post and left a massive dint. When it came time to return the car, quick thinking by Alan the photographer saw him stand in front of the dint while the hire car company attendant checked for scratches. Alan also suggested that we leave with the young lad from the car company all the samples of jamón and sherry that producers had given us. So, overwhelmed with dozens of bottles and kilos of top-grade jamón, he quickly gave us back the paperwork and hawked his stash back to his dark little office.

Frank, Cesc, Alan and myself said our goodbyes and headed off in different directions. I was catching up with a mate in Barcelona and then we were going to San Sebastian for a few days. My friend, Matt Dawson, is a chef originally from Wodonga and was travelling with his dad, John, who claimed he had eaten nothing more adventurous in his life than a parmigiana Mexicana. Matt and I gallivanted around San Sebastian, ordering way too much food, just so we could sample it and get an idea of how the dishes were put together. It's called culinary immersion education. The sliver of jamón having broken the seal, I was now in arguably the world's best city for food, and could pick and choose delicious little meaty morsels. A tiny piece of grilled steak at first, then some smallgoods and then some exquisite fish dishes. John didn't appreciate us leaving food on the table, so made a point of finishing up all the foie gras, lamb sweetbreads, ears, livers, razor clams, and other dishes quite unknown in the clubs of southern New South Wales and northern Victoria.

It was great having John with us, as he could spot culinary pretenders a mile off. We went to one Michelin-starred restaurant in San Sebastian, famed for its modernist cuisine. Afterwards, in the taxi back to town, he simply asked, 'What the fuck was that?' A case of the emperor's new clothes in practice.

There was one restaurant that struck a chord with all of us. It's up in the foothills of the Cantabrian Mountains, near Guernica. Asador Etxebarri is a simple but costly grill house in an old home in a village, surrounded by rolling hills and apple trees. Down under the home, in what was probably the pigs' winter quarters, is the kitchen of chef Victor Arguinzoniz. Here he makes his own charcoal from different types of wood, and gently grills meat, fish and vegetables over the glowing coals. It's good, honest and deceptively simple food that is served in a comfortably appointed dining room in the old-fashioned Spanish style, looking out over the village and the mountains beyond. Good bread. Smoked goat's butter. Grilled prawns. Grilled peas. Grilled steak. A slowly grilled rib eye steak from what Victor claimed was a 14-year-old dairy cow. Up in the north of Spain they don't eat a lot of yearling, the way we do in Australia. They like their steaks to have had a life of doing something else before they hit the plate. We'd call it ox. I'd call it the best steak I'd ever had. Lined with a strip of thick yellow fat, the flesh was deep red and interlaced with veins of now liquefied intramuscular fat. The aroma was of beef, bone, and was slightly lactic from the dry ageing, and there was a very faintly grassy floral note. Was it tender? No. The word tender is used in steak marketing to promote grain-fed beef that comes out of feedlots. Good beef should offer some resistance to the tooth but release moisture and flavour as it is chewed. Grain-fed beef is like the 1980s chewing gum Spurt, releasing a burst of fat into the gob then reducing to a gluey paste. Good beef requires teeth, and a knife and fork to cut it into three-quarter-centimetre slices on which the teeth can then do their work. Served with salt, this was the Platonic ideal of a steak. A benchmark that all other steaks would be compared to henceforth. John was so appreciative of the quality of the meal that, despite his lack of Spanish, he was able to convey his gratitude through rioja-induced mime, charm and use of schoolboy Italian. The matronly waitress was so impressed she sent another steak to the table. And didn't put it on the bill. That a steak that was so good came from an animal that had lived a full life reminded me of what dairy farmer Vicki Jones was trying to achieve with her herd of older dairy cows. People fly across the world to eat old-cow steak at Etxebarri. I hoped that Vicki Jones's experiment would succeed, so I could get old-cow steak in restaurants back home.

THERE'S NO PLACE LiKE HOME

I was back in Australia and 'back on the meat'. Not the bacon-devouring demon of before but a more disciplined and discerning diner who only ate a little top-shelf flesh. I had eaten the best and there was no return. I was also back doing my usual job of interviewing people about their produce and photographing them for *The Age Epicure*.

I heard that a couple of small-scale pig farmers were doing something special with their pigs by fattening them on acorns, like I had witnessed in Corteconcepción in Spain. I jumped in the HiLux and headed west towards the Grampians. If you haven't seen them, they are a spectacular sierra, 1000 metres high, 100 kilometres long, half a billion years old, rising out of the volcanic plains about 300 kilometres west of Melbourne. To the Djab wurrung and the Jardwadjali peoples these ranges are known as Gariwerd. The reason why this country was so attractive to the early settlers was the farming work the Aboriginal peoples had done with their firesticks. They had used them to create a patchwork of freshly burned and recovering grass, so the kangaroos would come and graze on the new green shoots. Daisy yams and orchids were dug up in summer, by the women, for their starchy tubers that were then roasted over the fire. The result was freshly turned earth recycling the carbon from the fires back into the soil. The region is interlaced with creeks and rivers, and was once covered in seasonal wetlands where the Indigenous hunters set their fish and eel traps, fished for mussels and hunted tortoises. I turned a corner and took the long gravel driveway to the Greenvale Farm homestead, where I would meet the interviewees for the story.

I first met Greenvale's owners Anthony and Amanda Kumnick around 2009. They had just arrived back from living overseas and were settling into their new lives as farmers. Anthony had worked hard in IT and saved enough to come back to the district he grew up in. Amanda was born in England's West Country. The Kumnicks bought Greenvale and its imposing sandstone homestead and, instead of raising sheep like every generation since Greenvale was first settled in the 1840s, they decided to raise pigs. Not a modern pig farm, with an isolated shed next to a feed silo and waste treatment pond. They wanted to raise pigs in the same manner as farmers had done prior to World War II. The pigs were to run free range in paddocks under the river red gums, with low fences to keep them from escaping. They were to be fed with grain grown mostly on the farm. They were to sleep in small huts made from either hay bales or sheet metal with a deep layer of straw litter.

As recently returned expats, the Kumnicks exuded energy and enthusiasm. Amanda has an infectious smile, and a wonderful turn of phrase delivered with the occasional elongated vowel from her West Country upbringing. As Amanda is loquacious, Anthony remains tacit. A man of few words, he retains his Western District demeanour of keeping his thoughts to himself until they are perfectly formed and really matter. That first time I met them I stayed on their farm with my young family. Our children fed the few house lambs from a bottle and poured buckets of feed into the troughs for the pigs, who grunted contentedly. We talked well into the night, drinking wine from the vineyards nearby. Amanda painted a picture of a farmstay B and B with a network of small producers like them that one could drive to and visit. They were going to sell their pork from the farm as well as at farmers' markets, cutting out the middlemen, to increase the margins for themselves. We ate their pork. It was roasted with a thick layer of salted crisp crackling. To this day I contend their pork is some of the best in the nation. Life that night was ideal. The Kumnicks knew they were in for hard work but what they didn't realise was just how hard life was going to get.

This time Greenvale looked very different. A tornado had torn through the farm the previous summer, ripping the top limbs off the ancient river red gums. Tornados were not unknown in this part of Victoria but they had never been this fierce. The weather had started changing. So had the farm. This broadacre grazing and grain property on the banks of the Hopkins River, not far from the Grampians, was looking a lot different. The operation was much larger than when I first visited. The pigs were still grazing under the old river red gums but there were more of them. They were still grazing in paddocks around the homestead but now there were another two paddocks in the farm across the road. The little houses of straw were now more sturdy galvanized iron sheds, shifted by tractor with a front-end loader. Anthony and Amanda had developed the brand further, with striking graphics on the packaging and a range of really good smallgoods.

Part of the herd was now grazing on a different property, near Dunkeld, where another grazier had planted thousands of oak trees.

The oaks were now mature and were dropping acorns. The Greenvale pigs were rooting about under the oak trees and getting fat on the acorns. The acorn-fed pigs were sent to Melbourne and butchered by an Italian family, who salted down the back legs and air-dried them for six months or more. The flesh inside was the closest thing to jamón I have ever had outside of Spain. It was ruby red with streaks of white fat between the muscles. The flesh smelled nutty, buttery like hot popcorn, minerally like wet ironstone. The fat was so well formed that it had a low melting point, like quality chocolate. After cutting a small piece off and placing it on the tongue, it felt cool, as heat was drawn from the tongue to melt the fat in the flesh. It was good. Really good. I made a note that they could sell this for hundreds of dollars a kilogram.

Anthony and Amanda had increased the farm in size and scale and they were now value-adding to their product, increasing its value and its shelf life. They were converting their crops on which their pigs fed to biodynamic practices. The Kumnicks were employing people, local people, to help on their ethical farm. The only thing was—it was no longer theirs.

We went back to their farm on the banks of the Hopkins. The tornado had missed the house and most of the outbuildings. Only one shed had a few pieces of twisted iron roofing. It was the old trees that had copped the brunt. Some were uprooted. Most were surrounded by the now brown and dry upper branches, lying on the ground like a demented autumn leaf fall. We walked around these as we inspected a herd of Tamworths. These are ginger pigs with a very pleasant temperament. 'Personality,' said the herd manager. 'When you work with pigs enough, you understand that they have personalities. Not temperaments. You get better results from your animals when you realise that they are all different and have different personalities.'

Amanda walked along the paddock, kicking little tussocks of grass as we went. 'Anthony and I had to sell the farm,' she said. It wasn't working out financially and they had some tensions with other family members. Like many Australian farms, Greenvale involved a few more family members than just the married couple. A few failed crops, financial stress, and the dream turned into a nightmare. The bank called in the loan and was set to sell their home, their land, and break apart the breeding herd, selling the fertile mothers for sausage meat. It was a harrowing time for Anthony and Amanda. They had arrived back feted but now they felt shame as farming failures. Those who have never farmed won't understand the relationship between a farmer and their farm. It's not only part of your identity, it is part of you, part of your psyche, and part of your soul. A farmer who has lost their land walks among the community like a leper. There's pity but also resentment and anger. Because it reminds the rest of the community of their own fallibility. Many farmers are just one bad season away from the bank manager or sheriff.

Just days before the bank was set to take back the keys to the front gate, Anthony did something truly remarkable. He jumped on the Internet and then the phone, and called everyone he knew and everyone he had heard of who not only had money but who had vision. Without pride, ego or a hint of shame, he hawked his farm and business around the financial centres. The quietly spoken pig farmer found hidden erudition when it came time to save his family's bacon.

A Melbourne family with a trust dedicated to ethical and sustainable endeavours bought Greenvale Farm. They understood the Kumnicks's vision and invested in the farm, keeping Anthony and Amanda on as managers.

'You want to eat sustainable food?' said Amanda, talking openly to me. 'Sustainable food means that there has to be something in it for the farmer. It doesn't matter how green or organic or touchy-feely or nice their story is, and how they are taking carbon out of the atmosphere and burying it in the soil; unless they are making a living, it is not sustainable. It can't go on if farmers are going broke. I can tell you that many of the farmers you see, you buy from and you write about at the farmers' markets and the likes, are doing it very tough. There's long hours, varying seasons that look like they are getting worse and just so much uncertainty. And what is the media's obsession with "small" farms? Yes, it's all very good to have small and ethical farms but if the farmers are not being paid properly, then that is not sustainable. Nor is it ethical. You don't write about the big farms. But they are part of the community too. They are our neighbours. We know one family who, thankfully, took out crop insurance. The season was beyond a joke and much of the crops they planted failed in the spring heatwave. They were paid out $1 million. That's just how much it cost to put their crop in! Imagine spending a million dollars not knowing if you're going to get a return or not. There's this focus on the small and cute but the reality is the broadacre carrot grower who sells to Coles. The prime lamb producer on 2000 acres. The dairy farmer with 250 milkers. These are people who are taking real risks, just like us. And you try and find a cattle, sheep or pig farmer who says they get better results by mistreating their animals. You can't. *All* farmers know that the humane treatment of animals is the best way of getting the best beef, wool, leather, pork, cheese, or whatever, from their animals. That is the real world of food. Big farms. Real farmers. Real people.'

The Kumnicks are continuing on their journey and will soon be 'closed circle' certified biodynamic farmers, meaning they will grow all the grain on their farm to feed their pigs. They still hand-sell their pork at farmers' markets and it is still some of the best on the market. Their plans are, however, to get bigger, increase the economy of scale, and improve the quality of the soil on the farm in the process. They are ambitious. And, knowing those two, they will achieve what they set out to do.

THE TROUBLE WiTH SMALL FARMERS

The meat I want to eat comes from small producers like Amanda and Anthony Kumnick. But it is bloody hard to get and it is costly. You can buy supermarket bacon for $7 a kilo. This is made in Australia from frozen pork from pigs raised in industrial farms in Denmark or Canada. It is greasy, watery, and when chewed reminds me of the sad, grey, joyless food George Orwell described in *1984*. The Kumnicks's bacon is wonderfully dense, flavoursome, meaty and has a buttery smoothness. It costs $32 a kilo. It is costly because of the inefficiencies in their farming systems, as agronomists would say. The farmers would say that the reason the food they produce costs more than the stuff in the supermarket is that it reflects the true cost of farming, when all the labour and the ethical methods of farming are taken into account. There are higher labour costs. Instead of premix pig pellets being sent via a pipe into the feed troughs of pigs, as it would be in a shed, there are people hand-mixing the feed and tipping it into their feed troughs. There are people on the farm who move the pigs from paddock to paddock. There are people on the farm who move the sheds in which the pigs shelter. There is not only more labour but fewer opportunities to gain economies of scale. Instead of one truck filled with hundreds of pigs, the animals are 'turned off' (sent away from the farm) by the dozen, if not fewer. The animals are slaughtered and butchered in small lots, which again presents administrative costs. This system is replicated for many small producers across the nation. There is a nascent movement to have on-farm slaughtering and butchery, which reduces transport and administration costs. It will be at least a decade, if ever, before we see on-farm slaughtering, but on-farm butchery has already started. In a nutshell, the above reasons are why the hams produced by farmers like the Kumnicks cost $200. You can have cheap ham from Canadian factory pigs for $50.

One of the biggest barriers to lowering the cost of ethical meat is the demands placed on farmers by state government regulators, such as PrimeSafe in Victoria, which enforces the Meat Industry Act. In New South Wales this work is done by the NSW Food Authority. The work done by this state body is similar to that of the authorities around the nation. The red tape, onerous testing regime funded by the food producer and negative attitude to small-scale butchery and processing is also to be found in all other states and territories. These government bodies have done a sterling job of protecting Australian consumers from a tragic situation that killed a 4-year-old in South Australia in 1995 after she ate defective salami. The measures put in place by these organisations mean our meat and smallgoods are free from harmful microbes. But in doing so they have created a culture that is aggressive towards small meat producers. In Victoria the environment created by regulation is so toxic to artisan meat production that many of that state's best small producers send their meat to New South Wales, Tasmania and South Australia to be made into smallgoods. There, meat production is still safe but much more conducive to small producers, and the smallgoods are fermented and sent back to Victoria to be labelled as local produce. This should be a warning to the rest of the country that a state authority is acting like a frontier sheriff, without the necessary ministerial oversight to keep it in check. Sometimes the situation seems Kafkaesque.

PrimeSafe oversees abattoirs, butchers, fish and poultry processors and meat delivery in Victoria. Most beef in Victoria is sold through the big two supermarkets, which buy meat from animals raised in feedlots, and, at the time of writing, Woolworths was still using hormone growth promotants in its cattle. Because meat is not their main businesses, however, supermarkets don't fall under the jurisdiction of PrimeSafe. Instead they come under the much less fearsome realm of local council health departments. PrimeSafe has developed a reputation for destroying meat, breaking open prepared salamis, and threatening a farrago of legal consequences when, without evidence or proper testing, they so much as suspect a butcher of making unlicensed salami. Inspectors have been known to pour bottles of a butcher's own cleaning fluid over meat or fish they thought, but had not proved, had breached their regulations. I have spoken with several butchers who tell the same story. I have been told butchers are instructed to sign documents declaring that they are guilty of transgressing the act and that they will not transgress again. This is a contract signed, it would seem, under duress and without access to legal counsel.

The way the state of Victoria has set up its meat industry regulator could not be more antagonistic to small producers if it tried. I have interviewed butchers who have wept at the unfair treatment that PrimeSafe dealt to them. One former butcher who was known nationally for his smallgoods recently closed his doors. I received a sad text from him: 'Richard. I can't take the BS and pressure from PS [PrimeSafe] anymore. It is killing me. I have to get out and do something else. M'.

PrimeSafe officers have worked against people who used to produce the best goods. There was a Spaniard, from Galicia, living near Geelong in regional Victoria ten years ago, who was making superb Spanish-style hams. They were close to Spanish jamón. He knew how to salt the hams, how to dry the hams; he knew how to manipulate the hams around the drying room to get the best result. His name was Angel Cardoso. Everyone who had been overseas and tasted jamón had lauded his jamón as being the real thing. But he was producing it outside PrimeSafe's regulations. PrimeSafe inspected him close to Christmastime one year and took away hundreds of thousands of dollars worth of his jamóns, disposing of the hams.

A recent guideline released by PrimeSafe saw the traditional practice of dry ageing meat in low-turnover butcheries virtually wiped out overnight. This is a process in which meat, almost universally beef, is hung in very cold storage for around thirty to sixty days, sometimes longer. During this period, enzymes in the meat break down the protein in the muscle tissues, making the meat tender. This is the process I've explained previously, when muscle sugar called glycogen is transformed by lactic enzymes into lactic acid. The result is a rich tasting and beefy piece of meat with a clean lactic finish. Traditional beef. The new PrimeSafe guidelines mean that this cannot be done unless there is frequent and costly testing, and unless the dry ageing occurs in specially created dry-ageing chambers, costing tens of thousands of dollars each; other states are not as draconian. These are regulations placed upon an industry that is struggling to survive in the wake of the supermarket juggernauts that regularly lower the public's expectations about the price and value of meat, by covering their advertising with massive pictures of $10 rump steaks. That is the marketing that is being forced on us: we expect meat to be cheap.

I watched one of Australia's best wagyu farmers struggle under this ham-fisted regime. Neil Prentice raises purebred wagyu on his farm in the hills above the Latrobe Valley in Gippsland. He farms using biodynamic practices, and his cattle are mostly pasture fed, with some additional grain mix towards the end of their three years. He used to make a wagyu salami. The testing became too expensive. He used to make wagyu bresaola. The testing became too expensive. He used to make the best dry-aged beef in Australia. His butcher couldn't afford the dry-ageing room. He still grows what I consider to be the best free-range wagyu in Australia.

The ridiculous approach taken to the interpretation of laws that are meant to protect our health has even more bizarre unintended consequences. One of the best free-range poultry producers I know has been forced into a farcical situation. They run their birds in large outdoor cages that are moved daily onto new pasture. The pigs follow the chickens several months later and turn over the new growth flourishing on the manure. The family have transformed a barren block of land, denuded by over a century of mining, and what was in places bare rock into arable land. What was ochre rock is now deep-green pasture. What was brown stubble is now flourishing multi-species pasture. The chickens act like real birds, and scratch and peck and spread their wings and do the occasional little fun run. Slaughtered at almost double the number of days the standard supermarket chook is knocked on the head, these are really tasty birds. They are so large, you can feed a family of four three times on one of them. Twice the weight of a supermarket chook, twice the price, but you get twice as many meals.

For the farmer in question, however, there is something very disconcerting about the bureaucracy surrounding their slaughter. Because they are so small there is no prescribed procedure that fits them. The farmer has to sign a document stating his birds are legally owned by the processor. The processor can then slaughter them, process the birds and hand them back to the farmer, who sells them at farmers' markets. It is bizarre. This is the way governments treat the people who feed us. People who practise some of the most sustainable farming techniques we have.

Some Australian farmers have taken a stand. There are small producers, like Tammi Jonas from Jonai Farms, who are fair farming advocates. She has a vision for a small on-farm abattoir and farm-gate butchery and shop. For her it's two steps forward, one step, sometimes two steps, back. An instance of this was connected to a salami education programme she held on her small free-range and ethical farm near Daylesford. She advertised the event and put up photos on social media. Shortly afterwards, inspectors came to her farm unannounced, and destroyed not only her own salamis made for her family, but all the salamis belonging to the other participants in the class.

It is sheer lunacy that the state government is stifling a huge latent demand for sustainable products that could see hundreds of jobs being created in small, and sometimes regional towns and communities. In this atmosphere, how does small artisanal meat production flourish? Imagine if thirty years ago the Australian Wine and Brandy Corporation was going to wineries and smashing barrels if the winemakers were using wild yeast or making wine from non-French varieties. We wouldn't have the flourishing, diverse wine industry we enjoy now. Even though it is just a handful of jobs in any one place, in a small town a few men or women holding full-time employment can mean the difference between holding onto or losing their schools, doctors, stores and other businesses. The rise of the small-scale farmer could see us eating exceptional meat but much less of it. Which would not be a bad thing.

MEAT SHOCK

In October 2015, twenty-two scientists from ten countries met at the International Agency for Research on Cancer (IARC) in Lyon, France, to evaluate the carcinogenicity of the consumption of red meat and processed meat. They determined that, from reviewing ten different studies, there was a statistically significant dose–response relationship between red meat consumption and colorectal cancer. They found a 17 per cent increased risk per 100 grams per day of red meat and an 18 per cent increase per 50 grams per day of processed meat.

It wasn't this World Health Organization (WHO) report that meat is linked to colorectal cancer that surprised me. That was old news. It was the public reaction to the report, indicating the issue is the global warming of health. There is a growing and alarming anti-science movement in which people don't want other people to tell them what to think, about anything. This is the way the anti-science conversation goes:

Scientists: Here is the information. Of the thousand scientists in the room, 999 agree the information is true.

Protagonist: Let the thousandth scientist speak. I wanna hear what he has to say.

Protagonist 2: Yeah. Let's hear it from the dissenter. He has something important to say that agrees with my well-formed opinion.

Scientists: But your well-formed opinion is not well informed.

Protagonists: But change is bad, and that scientist over there chewing on the charred hot dog looks like he has something important to say that I could possibly agree with.

What the study didn't say was that eating bacon was like smoking fags. Meat and preserved meat were classified by WHO as a Group 1 carcinogen, placing it in the same league as tobacco and asbestos. Australia's Agriculture Minister at the time, Barnaby Joyce, dismissed the report. 'If you got everything the World Health Organization said was carcinogenic and took it out of your daily requirements, well you are kind of heading back to a cave', he said. What the report did say was that meat is a dense source of nutrition, but eating too much of it raises your risk of getting colorectal cancer. And Australians eat way too much meat. The WHO report, published in *The Lancet Oncology*, stated that the global mean intake of meat is around 50 to 100 grams of red meat per person per day. The average Australian eats a whopping 185 grams of red meat a day. Australia also has, unfortunately, the eighth-highest rate of colorectal cancer in the world.

The report pointed the finger at high-temperature cooking, such as pan-frying, grilling or barbecuing, that produces known or suspected carcinogens, such as heterocyclic aromatic amines and polycyclic aromatic hydrocarbons. The report also stated that 'meat processing, such as curing and smoking, can result in formation of carcinogenic chemicals', which include nitrosamines and nitrosamides (NOCs). These occur when the preservatives that are added to processed meat, to make it safe from deadly bugs like the botulism bacteria, react with other compounds in the meat to create carcinogens. It is important to note that although nitrites and nitrates occur naturally in plants, including leafy greens, these plants also contain compounds that inhibit the transformation of the nitrates and nitrites into the cancer-causing NOCs. Heme iron, found in red meat, can help transform nitrites and nitrates into NOCs in the gut. For this reason, some people are choosing to avoid sausages, hams, bacon, pancetta and other smallgoods preserved with these chemicals, and are reducing their intake of red meat.

What the WHO report did not take into account was the consumption of vegetable fibre, and the time red meat spends in the gut. Good gut health is promoted by eating plenty of fibre-rich vegetables of different types and colours, and pulses and beans, as recommended by the Australian Dietary Guidelines. American food writer Michael Pollan put it best when he wrote in his book *In Defense of Food*:

Eat mostly plants, especially leaves. Treat meat as a flavouring or special occasion food. Eating what stands on one leg [mushrooms and plant foods] is better than eating what stands on two legs [fowl], which is better than eating what stands on four legs [cows, pigs, and other mammals].

There was so much teeth gnashing going on around this matter that I simply could not resist the urge to post this on Facebook at the time of the WHO report's release:

OK meat lovers. Keep your hats on. The final WHO report is not in but speaking to health professionals today my bet is to watch the research on red meat, watch the research come in on the time red meat spends in the gut. If red meat is eaten with loads of good veg then a swift movement through the gut will be healthy. Think a little bit of steak with loads of seasonal veg. Or a braise with, again, loads of veg. It's not proven yet but wait for the science to come in. I predict the old fashioned diet of seasonal veg and a little bit of meat will be justified. Until then, keep calm and eat a little bit of ethical meat and loads of seasonal veg. You'll feel better until you are proven right.

Here is an edited selection of comments I received in response to my post:

JH: As a Nutritionist I have to say there goes WHO cred.

HB: I suspect this all has more to do with the chemicals put into the meat rather than eating meat itself. So much crap added to mass produced products it's the same for other foods too. Processed convenience foods equals bad.

JH: I agree with HB and then there is meat itself (grass-fed, organic grain-fed etc) Point: The ONLY diet to be scientifically proven many times to be of health benefit is the Mediterranean. Which has processed and red meat in it—just how I like it!

CS: Eat more organic, grass fed meat. Ask your butcher if it's grain fed (organic does not mean grass fed just by the way!). And find a butcher that uses nitrate free, buy direct from the farmer, or from a butcher that does!

XP: https://www.facebook.com/xavimagik?fref=ufi   Thanks mate! I'll have an Angus scotch w asparagus and escalivada tonight at Las Tapas.

DB: Scaremongering.

DM: More bloody scaremongering.

NM: This sort of pseudo science drives me mad.

JC: I agree entirely with this. Obviously the reference to meat in the WHO report ignores well prepared and assorted meat such as the deliciously healthy Bollito Misto I once ate at a restaurant in Brunswick Street. Yummy and healthy!

JS: One of the WHO meat-cancer panelists is a rampant anti-meat vegetarian.

SC: Junk science.

ME: Oh dear God!

THINGS I LEARNED FROM MY YEAR WITHOUT MEAT

I am roasting a saddle of lamb. This is basically the lamb loin chops still on the spine bone. I have opened the cut-out, sprinkled the interior with salt and pepper, and trussed it up with butcher's twine. I've turned the oven on to 260 degrees Celsius and in it goes. For half an hour the fat under the skin will rapidly render into liquid oil and fry the skin. The skin will become parchment crisp and honey golden. Once this happens I turn the heat to 100 degrees and let the meat slowly reach a temperature of around 65 degrees, when the flesh inside will be pink. It weighs 2 kilograms and costs $35 a kilogram. It came from a Suffolk ewe, a black-faced sheep that grazed on land not far from the mouth of the Murray River near Meningie in South Australia. It is possibly the best lamb in the country. We are celebrating with family and friends tonight. After bone is removed and a lot of the fat rendered away, we will be left with 1.5 kilograms of flesh. Between ten of us that is under 150 grams each. Not a lot. But enough for it to look scarce on the plate and make us appreciate every mouthful. Served with exceptional wines and mounds of vegetable dishes, including parboiled potatoes roasted in the lamb fat, the meal will be a celebration of coming together, this book being finished, my partner's new clothes range and other life matters. Then that will be it for meat-eating for a while. We may have some fish, some egg dishes from the backyard chooks, but it will be a week or more before we have meat again. There could be a little bit of meat in a mostly vegetable curry, or perhaps some lamb in a ragout with lots of veg. We will have lots of mixed-vegetable meals made up from the fail-safe, all-bases-covered recipes shared in the next chapter.

For a long time, industry forces have promoted meat as the rockstar; as a result, too much attention has been given to the animal protein, and only diehard fans have remembered the vegetables on bass and the mushrooms on drums. After My Year Without Meat I realised that diet is an orchestra made up of so many different foods. You can decide if meat is your strings section, or the rarely used cor anglais or triangle. It depends on how you want to conduct your life.

We are at a point in our history when there has never been so much meat around us. Coles fired its first salvo in the supermarket price war with $1 milk. There was so little in it for the dairy industry they took their bat and ball and went to China, with the offer of lots of powdered milk. Now, local cheesemakers are struggling to find enough milk to make their cheddar. Another shot was fired with $5-a-kilogram beef mince. When the cost of an animal at market is around $5 a kilogram complete with guts, hide, bones and tail, you can see this is not sustainable. But to have meat offered at below the price of production lowers expectations and demeans all the social values around eating meat so much, that it transforms the way we perceive meat. With so much of it about at such low cost, I sometimes have a vision of humans being force-fed meat through a funnel, like French geese getting fattened for foie gras.

Once it is understood that at the heart of every mouthful of meat there is the forced, traumatic death of an animal, then we have no other option than to make important choices about what we eat. Once people like you make this connection, many choose the path of vegetarianism. That, for many, is the only ethical path. I have witnessed the perfect death of an animal, an assassin's bullet, coming from nowhere. 'The light gleams an instant, then it's night once more,' said Irish nihilist playwright Samuel Beckett. Meat from these animals tastes different. It tastes very good. I have decided to continue to eat meat. But not much of it. Just the best. Meat from people like the Kumnicks, from Vicki Jones, Lauren Mathers, Tammi Jonas. Fish from the local fishers. Oysters from blokes like Shane Buckley. It is because when it comes to what sort of meat we eat, if any at all, we have a choice. We have a choice over the life we live. Farm animals don't have that choice.

My Recipes

Sometimes during My Year Without Meat, my body would tell me what it wanted. 'You really should eat some spinach and brown rice,' it would say. So I made it. 'Tonight you should eat some pulses and greens.' So I would. Following are a handful of recipes for dishes that I cooked during that period. Some of them are really good for you. Some are just packed with ridiculous amounts of butter. All are really delicious.

MUSHROOM PÂTÉ

This is really good with pinot noir.

100 g butter or 100 ml extra virgin olive oil
½ onion, finely chopped
1 medium carrot, finely chopped
200 g mushrooms, sliced
1 teaspoon each of fresh rosemary and thyme leaves
salt and pepper, to taste
100 ml white wine
60 g sourdough breadcrumbs

Serves 4

Melt the butter or oil in a large heavy-based saucepan over medium heat. Add the onion and cook for 5–10 minutes or until golden. Add the carrot and cook for a further 10 minutes or until soft. Add the mushrooms, herbs, salt and pepper. Cook for 10 minutes or until the mushrooms are soft. Add the white wine and cook for a further 5 minutes to evaporate the alcohol. Add the breadcrumbs and stir.

Remove from heat and allow to cool a little. Place in a kitchen blender and blend to a smooth puree. Serve in a dish with slices of baguette, crackers or crudités.

BROAD BEAN PUREE

If you can be bothered, use twice as many broad beans, blanch them, double pod them by peeling the skin from the bean, then cook as below. The skin can be bitter but there is a lot of goodness in that skin.

100 ml extra virgin olive oil
1 clove garlic, finely chopped
400 g broad beans
salt and pepper, to taste
20 ml balsamic vinegar

Serves 4

Heat the olive oil in a large heavy-based saucepan over medium heat. Add the garlic and fry for a minute or so. Add the broad beans, salt and pepper and stir. Cook for 5–10 minutes or until the beans are cooked. Add the balsamic vinegar. Remove from heat and allow to cool a little. Place in a kitchen blender and blend to a smooth puree. Serve with toasted slices of sourdough.

CAPSICUM AND CASHEW DIP

A simple raw food dip that is really good spread on lettuce leaves and rolled up, then washed down with cold beer. The addition of a tinned chipotle chilli changes the story and makes a dip with a touch of heat.

1 red capsicum, chopped
200 g cashews
pinch salt
60 ml extra virgin olive oil

Serves 4

Place all the ingredients into a kitchen blender and blend until smooth. Serve as a dip or as a sauce for other vegetables.

TUSCAN BEAN PUREE

You know when a friend unexpectedly drops in for a glass of wine and you have no food in the house? There's a limp carrot and half a tin of dog food in the fridge and a cold bottle of verdehlo. This will solve that hospitality issue. It is so simple but bloody delicious.

1 tin cannellini beans, drained
50 ml extra virgin olive oil
¼ teaspoon fresh thyme leaves
pinch salt

Serves 4

Place all ingredients in a kitchen blender and blend until smooth. Serve with crudités (not a limp carrot) or crackers.

MiSO BUTTER

When you want something decadent with enough nutrition to justify the amount of fat you're mounting on your baked potato, hot carrot salad or sweet corn, then consider making some miso butter. This is really good to make in the Thermomix, if you have one, as it is so light. Michael Ryan of Provenance in Beechworth does the best version—his is smoked. It's amazing.

200 g unsalted butter, slightly softened
75 g miso

Simply mix the two together until blended. Lay out on cling film and roll up. Store in the fridge and cut off slices as needed. Will keep for several weeks.

CHiLLED ASPARAGUS SOUP

Delicious summer soup that is perfect with a little chilled sherry.

30 g butter or 30 ml extra virgin olive oil
2 bunches fresh asparagus, washed, trimmed, chopped
salt and pepper, to taste
600 ml hot goat's milk or vegetable stock
goat's fromage frais to serve
extra virgin olive oil to serve

Serves 4

Melt the butter or oil in a heavy-based saucepan over medium heat. Sauté the asparagus in the pan for 5–10 minutes. Season with salt and pepper. Add the goat's milk or stock and simmer very, very gently for 5 minutes. Remove from heat. Blend until smooth. Chill. Serve in bowls with a tiny dollop of goat's fromage frais and a little drizzle of oil.

ROMESCO SAUCE

It is funny the things one learns from research. During My Year Without Meat, I was asked to interview Ferran Adrià and provide a recipe of his that could be used at home. He was the wunderkind chef of the global molecular cuisine movement and based himself at his award-winning restaurant, elBulli, on the Catalan coast. I tried a recipe of his for romesco sauce. This is a great nut-based sauce that can be used with myriad foods but is great with all grilled vegetables. I discovered that the amount of vinegar his recipe asked for was out tenfold. The following recipe makes a much more palatable version of this delicious sauce.

500 g red capsicum
1 ripe tomato
3 garlic cloves
60 ml olive oil
60 g toasted blanched hazelnuts
200 g rustic bread, sliced
50 ml sherry vinegar
salt and pepper, to taste

Preheat the oven to 220°C. Place the capsicum, tomato and garlic in a roasting tin and bake for 45 minutes or until the peppers are blackened. Remove from oven. When cool enough to handle, peel the tomato and place the flesh in the bowl of a kitchen blender. Peel and de-seed the capsicum and place in the blender. Cut the heads off the garlic and squeeze the flesh into the blender. Add a tablespoon of olive oil to a frying pan over medium heat. Cook the hazelnuts for 4–5 minutes, tossing regularly until dark golden. Drain on paper towel. Add a little more oil to the frying pan and fry the bread on each side until golden. Break the bread into pieces and add to the blender, along with the hazelnuts. Add the remaining oil and sherry vinegar and blend to a rough paste. Season with salt and pepper. Store in an airtight container in the fridge.

PESTO

This is another great nut-based sauce, this time from Italy. The classic version is made with basil, pine nuts, garlic, parmesan and pecorino and is hand-pounded. The cheese adds the umami and extra virgin olive oil adds the moistness where required. Following is a basic recipe, but you can substitute different leaves, nuts and cheeses.

50 g bunch of basil (or parsley, rocket or a mixture)
60 g grated parmesan cheese
20 g grated pecorino
1 clove garlic, finely chopped
60 g pine nuts, toasted (or toasted hazelnuts, pecans or walnuts)
extra virgin olive oil

Except for the olive oil, place all the ingredients in a kitchen blender. Blend until a rough paste is achieved. Drizzle in enough olive oil, perhaps a few tablespoons, and blend until a smooth, but not uniform, paste is achieved. Serve a little over steamed or roasted veg.

MIGAS

A.k.a. Spanish breadcrumbs, these tasty little fellas make every steamed vegetable dish just that little bit more tasty. They are also great on pasta with broad beans, asparagus and fresh peas.

2 slices of 4-day-old sourdough bread
extra virgin olive oil to fry
3 cloves garlic, unpeeled
small sprig rosemary
sea salt flakes

You can break apart the bread with your fingers to create large breadcrumbs the size of something between a match head and a small Lego block. Or you can cube the bread and blend it in a kitchen blender to make rough breadcrumbs. Heat the oil to 170°C and add the garlic and rosemary. When the rosemary begins to brown, remove it and add the breadcrumbs and fry until golden. Remove from the oil and drain on a paper towel. Sprinkle with sea salt flakes. Serve immediately over vegetables.

RAINBOW COLESLAW

A mate of mine describes this salad coleslaw as being as colourful as a racing identity. This is a very colourful coleslaw and is good in baked potatoes with miso butter.

½ head red cabbage, finely sliced
2 carrots, julienned
2 Granny Smith apples, julienned
1 kohlrabi, peeled, julienned
20 mint leaves, roughly chopped
juice of 1 lemon
2 tablespoons extra virgin olive oil
1 teaspoon Dijon mustard
1 teaspoon tamari or Japanese soy sauce

Serves 4

In a large bowl, toss together the vegetables and mint. In a jar or bowl, mix the lemon juice, olive oil, mustard and tamari. With clean hands, dress the coleslaw, massaging the dressing in.

ZUCCHINI FRITTERS

500 g young zucchinis
salt
100 g feta
2 tablespoons self-raising flour
10 mint leaves, finely chopped
1 egg
olive oil to fry
natural yoghurt to serve

Makes 6

Grate the zucchini. Place in a bowl and sprinkle with salt. Set aside for 30 minutes. Pour the zucchini onto a clean tea towel. Gently squeeze much, but not all, of the liquid from the zucchini. Return to the bowl. Crumble in the feta, sprinkle over the flour. Add the mint leaves and crack the egg into the bowl. Using a fork, gently blend the mixture.

Pour a little olive oil into a heavy-based frying pan. Fry over a medium to high heat. Make fritters by gently placing about a tablespoon-sized portion of batter into the oil to make 6 or so. Cook for several minutes and turn when the base is brown. Cook for a further several minutes. Remove from heat and place the fritters on a plate lined with a paper towel. Repeat until all the mixture is used. Serve with natural yoghurt and salad.

LENTiL BURGERS

This is the recipe for the patties. I think you know how to assemble a burger. Toast the bun. Add a layer of mayo, lettuce, patty, cheese, sauce, onion, beetroot, pineapple, etc.

2 cups yellow dhal, raw
250 g sourdough breadcrumbs
1 tomato, chopped
20 basil leaves
1 teaspoon garam masala
2 eggs
salt and pepper to taste

Makes 12

Soak the dhal in a bowl of water for an hour. Drain. Place in a medium saucepan with 4 cups of water and cook over medium heat for 20 minutes or until the dhal is soft. Drain. Mix all the ingredients in a bowl (or blender). Using clean hands, form the mixture into 12 equal patties. Heat some oil in a heavy frying pan and fry each side for 5 minutes or until golden. Serve hot in a toasted bun with burger favourites.

RiCE AND LENTiLS

This is a dish of rice and lentils cooked together to make the easiest dish in the world for someone who wants to cook a fast, balanced meal. It's like the food you would get in a share house when the vego is cooking. Except tasty.

2 tablespoons olive oil

1 onion, finely diced

2 cm piece of ginger, peeled and very finely chopped

1 teaspoon turmeric

1 teaspoon coriander seeds

salt and pepper, to taste

1 cup rice

1 cup brown or red lentils

600 ml vegetable stock, hot

natural yoghurt, to serve

coriander, chopped, to serve

Serves 4

Heat the oil in a heavy-based saucepan over a medium heat and fry the onion for 5–10 minutes or until golden. Add the ginger and fry for a few minutes, then add the spices. Cook for a few minutes. Add the rice and lentils and stir. Season. Add the stock and add enough boiling water so the rice and lentils are covered by 2 cm of liquid. Increase heat to high. Bring to the boil and continue boiling until almost all the liquid has evaporated and there are holes left in the top of the rice and lentils. Do not stir from now on. Reduce heat to low, cover with a lid and allow to keep cooking for 5–10 minutes or until all the water has evaporated. The rice and lentils should now be cooked and no stock left in the saucepan. Serve hot with yoghurt and chopped coriander.

SAAG PANEER

Do you know in the world where the most cheese is eaten? France? The
United States of America? No, it's India. Soft curd and lightly pressed
cheeses are a staple for the nearly 1 billion or so Indians who eat dairy.
Paneer is a fresh cheese and has a soft but slightly chewy texture, like
barely salted feta. You can find it in Indian grocers. Or you can use
ricotta and squeeze it into balls to make little paneer nuggets.

3 tablespoons extra virgin olive oil (or ghee)

1 onion, finely diced

2 garlic cloves, finely chopped

3 cm knob ginger, peeled and finely chopped

2 teaspoons cumin seeds

1 tablespoon garam masala or curry powder

1 teaspoon turmeric

1 tomato, finely diced

500 g spinach leaves, washed and drained

60 ml cream

pinch salt

300 g paneer or soft cheese, like ricotta, portioned into 12 squares
    or dumpling shapes

Serves 4

In a large heavy-based saucepan, heat the oil, or ghee, over medium
heat. Add the onion and fry until golden, then add the garlic, fry for
a few minutes, stirring, then add the ginger, cumin, garam masala and
turmeric. Fry for a further five minutes. Add the tomato and cook for
a further 5–10 minutes until the tomato is soft and the contents of the
pan reduced. Add the spinach leaves, cream and a pinch of salt. Cover.
Reduce heat and cook for 5–10 minutes until the spinach is cooked.
At this point, if you like a smooth sauce, you can use a stick blender to
roughly puree the mix. Add the cheese and cook for a further 5 minutes.
Serve with brown rice.

GREEN BEANS, RiCOTTA AND MiNT SALAD

This is more a description than a recipe. It is especially good when the beans are young and the mint is tender. Even better if you can get your hands on some fresh ricotta.

600 g fresh green beans, topped and tailed
250 g fresh ricotta
20 mint leaves
handful of parsley, roughly chopped
lemon, juiced and zested
pinch salt
extra virgin olive oil to drizzle

Serves 4

Steam the beans for a few minutes or until just tender. Place on a serving plate and crumble over the ricotta. Tear the mint leaves and sprinkle over with the parsley, pour over a teaspoon of the lemon juice and lift through with clean hands to dress the beans. Sprinkle over a little zest of the lemon and salt and drizzle with a little olive oil. Serve warm.

HOT PANZANELLA

You know that great Italian salad made with fresh tomatoes and stale bread? This is what you do. You make double the quantity, and the next day you take the leftovers and bake them. The result is a beautiful rich savoury pudding. If you have a rustic *cazuela* that looks good on the table but can handle the oven, use it.

½ red onion, thinly sliced
8 ripe tomatoes, coarsely chopped
200 g 4-day-old sourdough bread, torn into walnut-sized pieces
4 tablespoons good wine vinegar
1 tablespoon capers
1 small clove of garlic, crushed
6 tablespoons extra virgin olive oil
small bunch of fresh basil, roughly torn

Serves 4

Put all the ingredients in an ovenproof dish. Mix well with clean hands. Cover with aluminium foil and refrigerate for 4–12 hours. Bring the dish out of the fridge and allow to warm at room temperature, so as not to crack the dish. Meanwhile, preheat the oven to 180°C. After 20 minutes, place the dish in the oven, covered, and bake for 20 minutes. Remove foil and bake for a further 20 minutes or until a golden crust has formed. Serve hot.

CAULiFLOWER CHEESE

This is a dish that says, 'It's winter. It's cold outside. It is only 5 p.m. but it's dull and there's no point going anywhere other than the kitchen and the dining room table. Open a bottle of pinot noir and stay inside.'

1 cauliflower, trimmed of leaves and excess stem
600 ml milk
3 bay leaves
½ teaspoon freshly grated nutmeg
30 g butter
2 tablespoons plain flour
100 g grated cheese, cheddar or similar
breadcrumbs and extra grated cheese

Serves 4

Bring a large pot of salted water to boil over high heat. When boiling, slowly submerge the entire cauliflower and cook for 15–20 minutes or until soft. Drain and strain. Meanwhile, make the cheese sauce by simmering the bay leaves and nutmeg in the milk for 15 minutes. Allow to cool a little. Make a roux in another saucepan: melt the butter and add the flour and cook for 5 minutes. Pour the milk over the roux and whisk thoroughly. Gently cook for 10–15 minutes, stirring continuously, until the sauce thickens. Preheat the oven to 180°C. Place the cauliflower in an ovenproof dish slightly larger than itself. Pour over the cheese sauce, sprinkle with breadcrumbs and cheese, and bake for 30 minutes or until the top is golden. Serve hot.

POTATOES iN WHiTE WiNE AND LEMON

This is a very simple way of making a very easy potato dish that is really good with brassicas of any sort: cabbage, brussels sprouts, etc. The top of the potatoes should be golden and underneath a lovely soft amalgam of creamy, soft, seasoned potato, onions and large chunks of firmer spud.

6 large potatoes, peeled and cut into large wedges

300 ml vegetable stock

100 ml white wine

juice of a lemon

1 tablespoon extra virgin olive oil

1 tablespoon each of chopped fresh parsley and oregano

salt and pepper, to taste

Serves 4

Preheat the oven to 180°C. Combine all ingredients in an ovenproof dish, cover with aluminium foil, and cook in the oven for 20 minutes. Remove cover and cook for a further 20 minutes until the crust is golden.

Acknowledgements

 I would like to thank Anita Simon and Mary Ellis for the use of their homes when writing this book. The team at MUP, especially Sally Heath for her ability to will a manuscript from another's being. He would also like to thank his long-suffering family, namely Tiffany, Ginger and Sunday.